ASTON MARTIN

HAYNES CLASSIC MAKES SERIES

ASTON MARTIN

EVER THE THOROUGHBRED

2nd EDITION

ROBERT EDWARDS

First edition published in June 1999
Second edition first published in August 2004

British Library Cataloguing in Publication Data:
A catalogue record for this book is available from the British Library

ISBN 1 84425 014 8

Library of Congress catalog card no. 2003110425

All illustrations by courtesy of LAT/Haymarket except where stated.

All databox prices are inclusive of purchase tax.

Published by Haynes Publishing, Sparkford, Yeovil, Somerset, BA22 7JJ, UK
Tel: 01963 440635 Fax: 01963 440023
Int. tel: +44 1963 440635 Int. fax: +44 1963 440023
E-mail: sales@haynes.co.uk
Web site: www.haynes.co.uk

Haynes North America, Inc.
861 Lawrence Drive, Newbury Park,
California 91320, USA

Designed and typeset by Drum Enterprises Limited, Ringwood, Hampshire BH24 4DL.
Material for second edition designed by Glad Stockdale.
Printed and bound in England by J. H. Haynes & Co. Ltd, Sparkford.

contents

Preface to the 1999 edition

John Bolster, that doyen of British motoring writers in the 1950s and '60s and constructor of the awesome 'Bloody Mary' special, who had the enviable job of road-testing motor cars before there was a speed limit, once described the Aston Martin as 'The Englishman's Ferrari'. He was, I am afraid, quite wrong. A Ferrari is Italian, and can never be anything else. An Aston Martin is British and can never be anything else. A Ferrari is Italian in the sense that Verdi, Puccini or Vivaldi were Italian. An Aston Martin is as British as Edward Elgar or Boadicea, with occasional and unavoidable overtones of Gilbert & Sullivan. Perhaps Henry Cooper in an Armani suit, for a while, but never quite Tommy Cooper; until you own one.

To me, Aston Martin have always made desirable cars. I first sat in one at the tender age of 14 or so when, close to our village, my brother and I discovered a sage by the name of Goldstone, who, it later transpired, was the local area rep for the Aston Martin Owners' Club, a happy band that I would join years later.

Mr Goldstone, from Cardiff and known locally, inevitably, as Auric, had, it seemed to me even then, known better days. He ran a modest garage and filling station near the village of Bradford-on-Tone in Somerset and there were usually a few fairly ratty examples of the marque parked in the back regions of his establishment. As schoolboys do, I asked him wise and penetrating questions: 'How fast do they go?' His reply, 'How fast do you want to go?' rather baulked me. I had no idea. I returned serve, with what I believed was Rod Laver topspin: 'How long do the engines last?' This would get him. I knew all about this. My father ran a Rover P4, which seemed, regrettably to me, to go on for ever. Mr

Goldstone repeated his answer to my first question.

How right he was.

What really struck me about the Aston Martins at Mr Goldstone's garage was, well, how basic they were. One was a light blue DB Mk III (as I discovered later), which had such thin seats that they could scarcely seem to be comfortable, but they were. Of course, these were not particularly old cars then, but I was also struck by their faded paint and what appeared to be very fragile bodywork. Weaned on cast-from-solid Rovers, you would be, wouldn't you? They had all led a hard life, were all kept outside and all ponged a bit, too. They seem to me now to have been rather closer to abused but patient mastiffs than once grand motor cars. They were all for sale, and seemed, I recollect, to average about £400 each. A lot of money in the 1960s, particularly if your income was restricted to pocket money.

Pleasingly we were invited to go for a spin. Never mind that we were clearly not potential customers, off we went. My brother sat in the front, grasping the grab handle (I had never seen one of those before) with his right hand and carefully cupping his genitals with his left, with me stuffed monkey-like on to the crude rear seat, head jammed against the roof for stability. He was a skilled driver, Mr Goldstone, and after a few miles, I was as hooked as any unwary catfish.

* * *

The years fall away and I am 43 as I write this, and frankly I have never aspired to ownership of one or any of these cars for any other reason than simply to partake of that unique set of experiences that clearly went toward creating them. Aston Martin

are, in more than one way, as British as Dunkirk or Rorke's Drift. It has not always been a happy association, and along the way I have owned many other cars – too many, really. Most of them bored me. Aston Martins do not. I am a fan, but not an uncritical one. If you like, I am a proud but serial victim. It has always struck me that whatever the shortcomings of an Aston Martin (and they are few), it has always been very clear indeed to me what it was that they were trying to do, which is not always the case in the making of cars. By and large, they seem to have pulled it off.

This assessment of the marque is, therefore, very much a personal one and not intended to be taken to heart. I hope that the information and opinion contained in it strikes a chord with those who either adore the cars, as I do, or have no particular opinion but merely seek information. For those who dislike them, I have no words of condolence that are adequate to convey my dismay at the condition of their miserable, rotten, politically correct, holistic, decaffeinated lives. But whatever I may say about the cars, and however flippant some of my comments about some of them may seem, please be advised that I find them totally beguiling. I merely feel that I have earned the right to comment.

Robert Edwards
Ditchling
East Sussex
1999

Preface to the 2004 edition

It is transparently clear that, since we left the story, the Aston Martin company has developed apace. Anyone who has followed the motoring press will know that it is a radically different company from that described in the first part of this book. As the first edition went to press in June 1999 the Vanquish was a one-off, possessed of a startling V12 engine. Logically enough we saw it first in a James Bond film, and from thence it has arrived among us. To see one on the road is to be struck not primarily by its great beauty, but rather by its understatedness.

In this second edition we move up to date with the Vanquish, the final developments of the worthy DB7, including the delicious limited-edition Zagato, and finally the DB9, a car so startling that it has left most commentators gasping, and is probably causing a few fundamental reassessments in Modena and Stuttgart as well. With the DB9, Aston Martin has moved into the universally-acknowledged front rank of car builders, a place where it has not necessarily always felt comfortable before.

I stated in my original preface that I liked Aston Martins for a number of reasons, but one of the chief ones was that it has always been clear to me what it was they were trying to do. The firm had never essayed the fastest car on earth (although they came close with the early AMV8), but rather they sought the best all-round package of performance, handling, comfort and safety. Despite the move to the extraordinary new headquarters at Gaydon in Warwickshire (near the Land Rover plant; the difference is obvious) that core objective – balance – is unchanged, and is clearly still a primary one.

Those who were worried that an Aston Martin would become a badge-engineered Jaguar were happily mistaken, and while it is clear that some of the back-of-a-fag-packet thinking of the 1950s went into that project, it was necessarily so; the Virage line, had it continued, would have sunk the company without trace, and not only because of the economic recession which plagued its arrival; the Virage, I am afraid, is not a very good car. It is far from a lemon, though, and many manufacturers would have been proud to build it, but it has come down to us as neither fish nor fowl – a Grand Tourer which is not quite sporty enough, and, that said, not really grand enough either. Throw enough money at it, however, and it is transformed.

It is also true to say that some people would never be happy whatever was served up, and there is no pleasing them; there is a bolus of diehards in every group of enthusiasts who will insist that the DB7 and all its iterations is but a warmed-over Jaguar, and up to a point that is true. But more importantly, it is a better car than any XJS ever was, and in V12 form it is arguable that it is a far better car than the XK8; for whatever you may think, it 'had the treatment'.

* * *

Since the first edition of this book was published a distressing number of people concerned with both the preparation of the cars, the book, or the history of the company have died; Walter Hayes, Victor Gauntlett, Roger Stowers, and Vic Bass have all gone, and although it will be small comfort to those they leave behind them, it is to their memories I dedicate this edition.

The works, now stretched somewhat to include the unique HQ at Gaydon, have, as ever, been most helpful, all the more so because of the magnitude of the efforts put in to ensure a smooth transition, even as I pestered them. Tim Watson, Peter Panarisi, and Chris de Vallancey, not to mention Barbara Prince (again), must be singled out.

Naturally, the reader will notice that I have not had hands-on experience of many of the newer Aston Martin models. I have not, for example, attempted to restore one, and all the indicators are that it will be a long time before I do. The reasons for this are not all economic either, as this latest generation of machines are clearly of an altogether higher order of reliability than that to which I am used, so I do not expect to ever be up to my elbows in 20-odd pints of over-exploited sump oil out of one of these.

The truth is, when I started to become interested in old cars it was generally because I could not afford new ones, and along that route I discovered some unique pleasures. I have to say that the prospect of resuscitating a 21st-century Aston Martin in 20 years' time is an altogether different prospect from keeping a terminally knackered DB4 on the road. Should it prove to be either necessary or possible, however, then I sincerely hope someone does it, for at least some of the reasons (not the financial ones) that I did; because, despite that fact that there is even a robot at Gaydon, there are people putting Aston Martin's together today who clearly do so with the same care and affection that they did when my own first DB Aston was pushed across the yard at Newport Pagnell to receive the first of its many engines.

Finally, it must be said; so much work has gone into the re-invention of the marque since I last wrote about it that these few pages can hardly do the vast effort sufficient justice, and for that I can only apologise.

Robert Edwards
West Sussex
2004

Aston Martin
introduction

Mergers are always difficult, the more so when neither company is quite the master of its own destiny. Both Aston Martin and Lagonda had enjoyed rather chequered financial histories, a fact that David Brown, the diminutive gear manufacturer from Huddersfield, found relatively easy to exploit when he acquired both firms after the war. Not that he had to haggle much: the prices were very low and both concerns were months away from liquidation. He had, by early 1948, captured them both for £72,500. One,

Aston Martin, based in Feltham, owned a very promising prototype, designed by a clever engineer named Claude Hill; it was called the Atom. The other, Lagonda, from Staines, a few miles down the road, had a very promising engine, fitted into a bulbous but rather accomplished car. This powerplant had been designed by one Willie Watson under the eye of W. O. Bentley. Known as the LB6 (Lagonda-Bentley six-cylinder), it was designed as a 2.3-litre, although it never ran as such, and later became a 2.6 twin-cam straight-six.

A pre-war sports Aston: a long-chassis 1½-litre Mk II of the 1934-5 period, powered by an ohc 1495cc 'four'.

KSU 893

At Lagonda the accent had been on properly built grand tourers and substantial sports cars. At one end of the spectrum, the mighty Meadows-engined 4½-litre Lagonda, bodied both formally and rakishly, had, since the demise of Bentley Motors, defined the ideal of the well-heeled pre-war

Aston Martin's aim was to make small-engined sports racing cars

motorist, and was a car which to our eyes is splendidly caddish. At the other, the tiny 1100cc Rapier, in many ways a gem of a car, had been the firm's attempt to widen its appeal without going noticeably down market. It was a worthy and prescient objective, and one with which the company's American founder, Wilbur Gunn, would have heartily approved.

Hailing from Lagonda Creek, Ohio, he had, sadly, died in 1922 and the firm had switched away from sensible, well-built competent cars (which sold well all over the world) toward a more Bentley-like approach in the rarefied atmosphere of the top end of the market. The Bentley concern had been a very early casualty of the Depression, dropping like a poleaxed steer into the waiting hands of Rolls-Royce in 1931. Thus it was only appropriate that when Lagonda Motors went the same way in June 1935, a consortium that included the great W. O. should bid for the assets, including the name.

The impact of the Depression was huge; not only was there no room for two manufacturers of the quality of Bentley and Lagonda, there was really not room for even one. After the dust of the stock market crash had settled, however, it became clear that there was a chance of some recovery. Pleasingly the consortium, led by Alan Good, had outbid Rolls-Royce, but

The C-Type was an attempt to update the pre-war 2-litre Speed Model by giving it semi-streamlined bodywork.

The car that gave its engine to the DB2 series of Astons: the Bentley-designed Lagonda, here in 3-litre drophead form.

ironically the tender process had opened on the Tuesday immediately after a Lagonda 4½-litre had won the Le Mans 24 hours race. In third, and winning the Index of Efficiency (a class designed by the Automobile Club de l'Ouest so that little French cars would usually win something) was an Aston Martin.

The re-invention of the Lagonda firm spelled the end of the delicious little Rapier. It lived on for a while, produced out of old stock by Rapier Motors Ltd, a doughty band of enthusiasts, but at Staines LG Motors (Lagonda/Good) settled into a business plan whereby engine capacities, power and prestige (and consequently borrowings) would all start to head north.

For a while it worked, culminating in the superior 4½-litre V12 engine designed by Walter Bentley, which was in production by late 1937. Now he was back in competition with Rolls-Royce: Lagonda V12 versus Phantom III. Probably as good as a Royce (if not a Packard), the Lagonda V12 marked a high-water mark of technical development for both Lagonda and Walter Bentley.

The war years revealed the flexibility of Lagonda's engineering heritage: gun carriages, oil engines, generators, compressors, aero-engine components and military sighting gear were all produced by Lagonda or its associates (they actually expanded a lot during the war), with the result that when hostilities ended the firm was left with huge spare capacity and fixed costs that simply gobbled up capital. Steel shortages and rationing didn't help, either.

At Aston Martin, meanwhile, they had never built an engine of greater than 2 litres, or with more than four cylinders, and their target was to produce small-engined, well-handling and efficient sports cars with which the happy owner could go racing when it suited. They had done well in competition and produced a series of cars that had, for a while, become almost the acme of their class. They had, it should also be added, seldom if ever made a profit. Build quality saw to that.

The firm had been founded in 1913 as Bamford & Martin Ltd. Robert Bamford and Lionel Martin had met as members of a cycling club in 1905 and went into the motor trade together in Fulham, where they acquired a reputation as tuners of Singer-engined cars. Later, in premises in West Kensington, they built their first car. It was a Coventry-Simplex-powered special, using a 1908 chassis by Isotta-Fraschini. They

christened it the Aston-Martin, naming it after the then famous hillclimb near Aston Clinton in the Chiltern Hills – there never was a Mr Aston. Their partnership was not to last, and Martin bought out Bamford in 1922.

Money was always very tight and only an injection of capital by Count Louis Zborowski saved the firm. By 1924 Lionel Martin had been supporting it via his own means, which were not infinite, and the death of Zborowski in a racing accident meant that the company needed to be refinanced. John Benson, later Lord Charnwood, obliged, but he and Martin were to fall out later, and after being placed into receivership the company came under the control of the Charnwood family.

By October of 1926 the Charnwood interests had been sold to Renwick & Bertelli, a recently formed Birmingham engineering company. The price was £4,000, which included the services of Benson. Renwick & Bertelli had designed an overhead-cam engine that was to be marketed to manufacturers, and they decided to develop the Aston Martin marque using this as opposed to the side-valve unit used by Lionel Martin. It was in all ways superior and was to prove to be very reliable. The Birmingham company decided to relocate southward and found a works in Victoria Road, Feltham. They brought with them a junior draughtsman, Claude Hill. There were, in fact, two Bertelli brothers, Augustus and Harry, and Harry came too, setting up his modest coachworks next door, whence came a series of delicious styles of body.

Renwick & Bertelli parted company about a year later and Aston Martin entered another volatile period; several investors stumped up, but the Wall Street crash and the resulting Depression made things very difficult indeed, and Bertelli apparently found it particularly hard working with Gordon Sutherland, the son of the

biggest investor. Bertelli had not, after all, been an investor himself, and, when all was said and done, this was supposed to be a commercial enterprise. He resigned in 1936, leaving the firm in the control of the Sutherland family.

After Bertelli's departure Aston Martin Ltd rather lost its way. The 1½-litre cars that he had developed had

It was the Atom that really made up Brown's mind – he thought the handling superb

sparkled in competition and, the not unassociated financial worries aside, the marque was now established as a major specialist manufacturer in an industry decimated by recession. Then came the war.

Aston's war years were spent making both tooling and the fiddly bits for aircraft joysticks, mainly as a subcontractor for Vickers at Brooklands. Meanwhile the cottage industry nature of the business allowed Claude Hill to develop his beloved saloon, the Atom, albeit on a shoestring, while war was raging. Over at Staines, however, Watson and Bentley were putting their final touches to the engine that would be Hill's professional nemesis at Astons.

Brown bought Aston Martin first. He did not seek it out; the Sutherland family advertised it for sale in *The Times*. He went to Feltham in the winter of 1946 to have a look, drove the Atom away and played with it for a few days while he thought about the acquisition. In the end, in February of 1947, he parted with £20,500 (the asking price was £30,000) and bought the company. It was the Atom that really made up his mind. He thought the handling superb, but perhaps

Sir David Brown

An earlier David Brown had founded a general pattern-making business in 1860, and one of the specialities of the firm became the making of patterns for cast gears. This led to the field of design and manufacture, and by 1873 the firm was making spur, skew, bevel and eccentric gearsets, all from castings, for applications in textile mills and heavy industry. By 1898 they were major manufacturers of machine-cut gears, and the gear-cutting business started to dominate the firm's activity. David Brown had three sons, Ernest, Percy and Frank. Upon his father's death in 1903, Percy became Chairman and Frank Managing Director. Ernest, the eldest, preferred the production side. The firm went from strength to strength during the Great War as makers of drive-trains for warships, gun elevation systems and assorted other military hardware, and by 1921 they had become the largest manufacturers of worm gears on the planet.

Percy Brown died in 1931 and his brother Frank succeeded him as Chairman. Frank's son David, born in 1910, became Managing Director, and the company consolidated throughout the Depression before producing its first tractor in conjunction with Harry Ferguson in 1936. At the same time they patented the Merritt-Brown caterpillar transmission, for use in both bulldozers and tanks, so they were in an enviable position at the outbreak of hostilities in 1939. The firm was also tasked with co-ordinating heavy military transmission manufacture by all other major British firms in the period prior to the Second World War under the Ministry of Supply.

David Brown bought Aston Martin and Lagonda personally, but as the DB industrial group was family-owned, the distinction was purely an accountancy one. By 1951 an automobile gear division was established at the Park works in Huddersfield, which became a major supplier to not only Aston Martin Lagonda but also the broader

European motor industry. The engineering traditions of the David Brown group were well established, particularly in the field of transmissions: a firm that could engineer the reduction gears for a 'Dreadnought' Class warship, handling some 120,000 shaft horsepower, would have no difficulty in making tiny gearboxes for 200bhp racing and road cars, or so it seemed. Ironically, the Brown-built transaxles on certain of the DBR racing cars would always be their Achilles' heel.

At the same time as Aston Martin was sold to Company Developments in 1972, the tractor division was disposed of to Tenneco, later to become a subsidiary of JI Case. Despite this, David Brown will always be remembered as a tractor-maker rather than the most successful of Britain's specialist engineering companies.

David Brown became a tax exile in Monte Carlo in the late 1960s as tax rates accelerated to ridiculous levels, and in 1990 the family interests were sold in a management buyout, funded by venture capital. In 1993 the group was floated on the London Stock Exchange, and became a public company for the first time in 133 years. That year Sir David Brown died.

the little four-cylinder engine was a trifle gutless.

Initially he did little with the company; he was too preoccupied with rebuilding the David Brown gear and tractor divisions to devote too much attention to his new toy. Indeed, he eventually might have gone down in history merely as one of the succession of owners before passing it on.

In Bradford, however, which was Brown's stamping ground, the local Lagonda agent was Anthony Scatchard, who was also a friend. The immediate post-war plight of Lagonda had been a cause for concern to its distributors ever since VJ Day, and Scatchard revealed that the firm was to be wound up and, not entirely out of self-interest, urged Brown to buy it. He revealed that the other parts of Lagonda, which had been developed during the war, such as the stationary engine and compressor concerns, had been hived off to Alan Good, who had lost interest in cars. The rump, once the core of a fine business and a fine product, was short of money, materials and leadership; it had been struggling.

But even in this reduced state, Lagonda was a very big-ticket item indeed. Brown actually knew the receiver well, and discovered casually that there were already three bids for the firm, from Jaguar, Rootes, and Armstrong-Siddeley, the highest one being £250,000. He shook his head. In receiverships, of course, time is of the essence to the seller. No one has to buy anything, so nobody hurries to do so, and a Dutch auction can often be the result. Happily for Brown, and unhappily for the creditors of Lagonda, the newly announced policy of Labour Chancellor Stafford Cripps, that the way forward was clearly wholesale nationalisation of the means of production, caused all three bids to melt away overnight. Nobody was prepared to bet that the cost of their investment would be supported

by a subsequent compulsory purchase. First, the government was functionally broke, far poorer than industry, and second, the very policy seemed to suggest that profits were obviously to be at the behest of the drab regiments of central planners, which fertile imaginations were conjuring up within hours of Cripps's 1948 budget statement.

Cleverly, on the basis that not even Labour could nationalise property (oh yeah?), the real estate element of the Lagonda company was stripped out and offered for separate redevelopment, which rather meant that the other assets and goodwill of the company were of little use to anyone who was not already a motor manufacturer and, for choice, a local one. Obviously, this narrowed the field, more or less to one.

Upon invitation, Brown went back to the receiver, who was becoming just a little sweaty by now, and further discovered that there was now only one new bidder in contention, and the best price was £50,000 without the factory. It was extremely hard to believe that the Staines works site alone was worth £200,000, vast though it was, so this seemed like something of a bargain. Brown smartly offered £52,500, and the goodwill, plant, current assets and Lagonda name were his. He did not need the works anyway; he had already obtained a suitable site just down the road. Thus it was that Aston Martin Lagonda was born, but it was not yet christened.

More or less straight away there were cross-cultural problems that Brown initially did little to correct. There were unavoidable job losses, for example, as a result of duplications. Claude Hill, who had been operating on a shoestring, looked forward to some decent investment in his engine. He was no stylist – a succession of efforts culminating in the Atom had demonstrated that – but Lagonda's Frank Feeley was; the Atom was

placed under a dust-sheet in a corner as a retired development hack, and work commenced on a new model. Feeley was actually out of work at the time of the Lagonda takeover, a casualty, like Walter Bentley, of the uncertainties of the period. Brown recalled him.

The car used a version of Hill's chassis and engine, but was clothed in an attractive drophead body designed by Feeley in something of a hurry: it went from crude sketch to production in 11 months. It was possessed of some pre-war Lagonda styling clues – indeed, rather more of them than was the case with the new Lagonda. It was called, however, the Aston Martin 2-litre. Only in retrospect would it be ever be called the DB1.

It was a pretty car, this. The long, flowing wings that had characterised Feeley's pre-war work were back, and the bonnet, although much longer than it needed to be, reflected the proportions of the grand routier machines that had been the previous staple of the Lagonda company. The rear end, with its well-defined haunches, could have been lifted straight from the immortal Rapide.

The car was thus a sort of pastiche of all the major Feeley styling themes and, while it had visual impact, one has the feeling now that one had seen it all before; the more so when the frontal design was effectively copied by Rootes for the Sunbeam-Talbot Alpine. In fact, the influence of Feeley's design can be seen in a whole series of Rootes products later. Not plagiarism, merely flattery.

Aston Martin
DB1

In production from September 1948 to May 1950, only in retrospect was this the DB1. It was launched as the Aston Martin 2-litre Sports and was the result of a speedy amalgamation of the complementary skills that Brown found he had acquired. The chassis was a longer version of the one designed by Hill for the Atom, the difference being that the rear springs were coils rather than the semi-elliptic leaf springs used on the dumpy prototype. At 9 feet (2.74 metres), the wheelbase was the longest of any Aston Martin (but not Lagonda) ever built.

Clearly Frank Feeley enjoyed styling this car; one has the sense that he dashed it off and it reflected all he knew. Freed from the constraints of the Lagonda styling brief, he reverted to the themes that had made him one of the pre-eminent pre-war stylists: huge, sweeping wings and a long, cavernous bonnet. The car looked as if it must have at least a Lagonda V12 in the engine bay.

Inside, however, was Claude Hill's little 1970cc four-cylinder pushrod engine, putting out a respectable 90bhp with a 7.25:1 compression ratio. That there was clearly space for something larger was not lost on Hill, but he had yet to discover fully the extent of Brown's intentions concerning the LB6 engine.

Only 14 cars were made, 13 of them dropheads. Clearly, from what was to emerge from the DB1, the chassis was a brilliantly clever piece of design and one cannot help wondering why it was that the Lagonda marque did not also employ it; instead, the

The complete DB1 car. Styled by Frank Feeley, it was elegant and surprisingly sprightly.

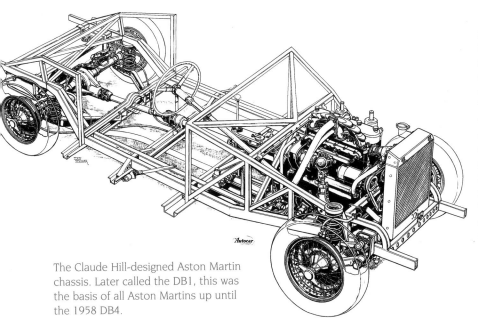

The Claude Hill-designed Aston Martin chassis. Later called the DB1, this was the basis of all Aston Martins up until the 1958 DB4.

Lagonda was built around a relatively crude cruciform frame that had to be strengthened substantially before volume production could begin. Perhaps it was out of deference to W. O. Bentley, but there can be no doubt that the Hill chassis was one of the best in the world at the time, and, had a version of it been applied to the Lagonda, that car would have been both lighter and quicker.

But only as a closed car. The DB1 did suffer from the removal of the roof in the sense that it was the roof that really squared the circle of rigidity. Rather as the perfect spaceframe is an egg, or an orb, the removal of the upper structure caused weaknesses to emerge, one of the main reasons why its successor was a closed car, and also lighter.

The first outing of Hill's chassis and engine were at the Spa 24-hour race in July 1948. After extensive testing in bare chassis form by St John Horsfall, the car was hastily bodied and despatched, with Leslie Johnson as co-driver, to make its slightly speculative debut. To everyone's amazement, the car won. Hill was delighted, of course. A version of the car that he had designed as a utility saloon had done the impossible. He

looked forward to developing a more powerful version of it.

The 'Spa special', as it became known, was never put into production, but merely used as a lure at the 1948 London Motor Show alongside its roadgoing sister car. Its price – £3,000 – more or less assured that it would not sell like hot cakes, but the publicity of winning the race was priceless. Spa was Aston Martin's first ever outright win in a 24-hour race, although of course Augustus Bertelli's cars had shone in class wins before the war at Le Mans. The heritage of Hill's engine was definitely from a sound line.

I had a rare opportunity to try the Claude Hill engine in the chassis for which it was built. Any reservations I had about the chassis were dispelled very quickly; the surface was by no means billiard-table-smooth, and while there was a measure of scuttle shake, the car felt sure-footed, even agile. The slightly bulbous styling does not assist placing the car, but as a swift tourer it is extremely accomplished. But bearing in mind the huge cost of the DB1 when new, so it damned well should be.

Hill's engine is very pleasing; throttle

response is first-rate, and bespeaks very little flywheel inertia. Its appearance is odd, however, with an exhaust manifold that looks, for want of a better image, 'back-combed'. The power is certainly strong and willing and the gearbox is, as far as I could tell, baulk-free. Mind you, I cannot imagine that the car was this swift when new; the petrol available then can hardly have enhanced matters. The steering is, if anything, too light, with a vagueness when going straight that is not assisted by skinny tyres.

Exploring higher rev ranges, I should imagine that this car could be hustled along quite happily using only third and fourth gears. It seemed at its happiest over about 3,000rpm. Overall, it is a little undergeared on a 4.10:1 axle, but that observation

As a test-bed the DB1 was very significant

must be put in context: the roads of the late 1940s were not, with a few notable exceptions, designed for prolonged high-speed cruising. A longer-legged axle would extract acceleration penalties, and this car is not exactly a dragster anyway. Overdrive is what it needs, I think. It is a nice car, and although it is extremely rare, the intelligent chassis and supple suspension were very much the shape of things to come. As a test-bed, the DB1 was a very significant car and I liked it a lot.

Compare this car to a Daimler Special Sports, for example, which is a reasonable parallel, and it has an altogether more modern feel. It looks much heavier than it is, and can even, under certain circumstances, be chucked around a bit. Try doing that with a Daimler and the tyres will give out a maidenly squeal, and you, unlike the car, will probably find yourself in traction.

Aston Martin DB2

In some ways it is a pity that David Brown decided to replace Claude Hill's engine with Watson's for use in this model, as in reality the LB6 engine was not really proven, whereas Hill's was, at least in four-cylinder configuration. Its specific output was relatively high, its architecture relatively simple and its lineage established; it looked to the high-output pre-war Aston units for its inspiration, and its performance at the Spa race had been encouraging. After all, it was almost indistinguishable from the engine of the hideous but worthy C-Type sports, which had been in production until 1940, when the imperatives of war manufacture had taken over. But Brown had not bought Lagonda in order to produce bank managers'

cars like the first post-war model; he had, in the inverse of his judgement about the Atom, liked the engine, but was neutral about the bulbous styling and felt that the oversteering car, all 1½ tons of it, was too heavy; and as anyone who has driven one will tell you, he was right. Despite this clear warning, Hill's confidence was high.

Not so Brown's. He abandoned the Claude Hill engine on account of its appearance as much as anything else; it was simply not exotic enough. Jaguar had already unveiled their twin-cam XK engine, which, rather like the cars themselves, was perhaps a little over-presented, but it certainly caught the eye. Its specific power

An early DB2: note the heavy side vents. This car, VMF 65, was ultimately re-engined with a DB3S engine.

output was relatively low, however, having been conceived, like the LB6, as a saloon car engine, but it was Jaguar's decision to put the XK120 into production in 1948 that probably tipped the balance as far as Brown was concerned.

Hill resigned. There is some suggestion that he might have stayed, but was urged to go by the combined efforts of St John Horsfall and Tony Rolt. Whatever the reality (and memories fade), it was not enough for him that his chassis was to be developed and applied in the new

Three men now joined the firm who would lead its development

car; he had set his heart on improving and refining his engine, but Brown was adamant, and Hill went. He moved, in fact, to the Ferguson concern, so still maintained a link with tractors, as it were, and latterly built a fine reputation in the industry for the work he carried out on the Ferguson four-wheel-drive system, later applied to the Jensen FF and also used by Ford.

But 1950 was a momentous year for Aston Martin. Not only was the DB2 launched, but also a succession of people joined the firm who were to have a profound effect on its evolution. First was John Wyer, who had been a partner at Monaco Motors in Watford, a race preparation company; he was to stay for 13 years. The second was Harold Beach, who arrived in September as a junior draughtsman and stayed for 28 years. The third was Dr Robert Eberan von Eberhorst, who stayed rather less time, only three years, for reasons that will probably become clear. By the end of the year, Aston Martin Lagonda was off and running.

Aston Martin DB2
May 1950–April 1953

ENGINE (Standard LB6/B):
In-line six-cylinder, iron-block

Bore x stroke	78 x 90mm
Capacity	2580cc
Valves	Twin ohc
Compression ratio	6.5:1
Carburettors	Two 1.5in SUs
Power	105bhp at 5,000rpm

TRANSMISSION:
Four-speed manual David Brown gearbox with synchromesh on all gears
Final drive   3.77:1 (standard) 3.5:1, 3.67:1 and 4.1:1 optional

SUSPENSION:
Coil springs all round.
Front: Trailing links
Back: Live rear axle with parallel arms supported by a Panhard rod
Steering: Worm and roller

BRAKES:
12-inch drums

WHEELS:
6.00 x 16-inch

BODYWORK:
Separate steel body and chassis

LENGTH:	13ft 6½in (4.13m)
WIDTH:	5ft 5in (1.65m)
WHEELBASE:	8ft 3in (2.51m)
HEIGHT:	4ft 5½in (1.36m)
WEIGHT (dry):	21.9cwt (1,112kg)
MAX SPEED: 0–60mph (97kph)	117mph (188kph) c11 seconds
PRICE NEW:	£2,000

LB6/E ENGINE (export):
As LB6/B except:

Capacity	2580cc
Compression ratio	7.5:1
Carburettors	Two 1.75in SUs
Power	116bhp at 5,000rpm

LB6/V & VB6/V ENGINE (Vantage):
As LB6/B except:

Capacity	2580cc
Compression ratio	8.16:1
Carburettors	Two 1.75in SUs
Power	125bhp at 5,000rpm

PRODUCTION FIGURES:
409, including at least 102 dropheads and 5 sold as chassis only
Chassis numbers: LMA/49/1 to LML/50/406 and LML/50/X1 to LML/50/X5

NOTES:
Several cars will now be found with non-original engines, not only because they came unstitched regularly when new, but also because copious supplies of Lagonda units are available. The originality brigade (see Lagonda chapter) are of the opinion that this is a sacrilege on a par with Charles V's sack of Rome. Personally, I think that the engine goes better in a DB2. Mind you, a BMW 325 engine drops in rather nicely as well. Just joking.

Later DB2 bodies were made by Mulliner in Birmingham. There were labour relations problems at Feltham early on in the DB2 run, and Brown was not about to put up with them.

Harold Beach

Beach joined Aston Martin in September 1950 as a design draughtsman after a career that had spanned working for Barkers, the coachbuilders; William Beardmore, the commercial engine manufacturers; and war work for the Hungarian Nikolaus Straussler in Park Royal. Straussler was a specialist in multi-wheel-drive layouts for military vehicles: the Alvis Stalwart design was originally one of his. Beach's starting salary at Feltham was £11 per week.

Claude Hill had left, and work was commencing on the successor to the DB2; the arrival of von Eberhorst ensured that the developments in trailing link suspension continued, not to everybody's satisfaction. Beach recollected being hopeful of designing a more modern wishbone layout, but was thwarted by von Eberhorst.

The Beach designs for the DB4, fitted with Marek's engine, were initially rejected by the Touring company and Beach had to redesign the whole chassis as a platform, which he did by the summer of 1957, by which time he was Chief Engineer. The car was ready by Christmas of that year and launched in October 1958 to critical acclaim. He incorporated his wishbone suspension, but could not use a de Dion rear axle – the David Brown gearbox was, while robust, too noisy.

Ten years later, Beach redesigned his chassis to underpin the DBS, and ten years after that adapted it to create the V8 Volante, his last project for Aston Martin. In April 1978 he retired. A modest man, his demeanour hid a steely determination. Virtually every innovation designed by him eventually found its way into production. A patient, precise and skilled engineer.

I do not have a particularly soft spot for the LB6 engine that replaced Hill's, at least not in its original form; even a cursory glance at some original factory service records can tell the tale: 'New engine at 4,000 miles, again at 12,000.' Appalling. Like the Lagonda racing V12 that was to come later, the early LB6 engine, particularly when compared to the offerings from Jaguar and Alfa, was clumsy, finicky and, if service records are any evidence, fragile. The reason was basically Watson. He had tried and failed with this layout on the Invicta Black Prince before he joined Lagonda, and was simply determined to make it work.

The key to the problem was the method by which the crankshaft was carried in its (inadequately few) four main bearings. The front main was conventional, but the other three were an extraordinary confection of huge split alloy 'doughnuts' that had to expand on to the iron crankcase as well as the iron crankshaft as the engine warmed up. Well, you can

A standard DB2 interior.

imagine. Aston Martin was always to have some conceptual difficulty with the problems caused by the differential coefficients of linear expansion; in an engine that was going to have to work so hard for its living, the resultant need for huge oil pressures was to be a distinct disadvantage. However, in the case of the DB2 series it was the only disadvantage of any real consequence, and was partially offset by the glamorous noise that the unit produced.

The DB2 was undeniably beautiful. It was a less flamboyant car than its predecessor and the appearance owed much to late-1940s Italian influences, a theme that began with this car. Frank Feeley's pre-war Lagonda work had rather defined the genre of the booming 1930s grand tourer; the influences brought to bear upon him now after a trip to Italy were to produce a car that was

The Watson-designed DB2 engine. Apart from the air cleaner, it is almost identical to the contemporary Lagonda unit, and for this reason many Lagondas have been cannibalised for spares.

delicate, refined and distinctive and owed much, externally at least, to the work of the Touring company in Milan, and which had been seen on chassis as diverse as BMW, Alfa Romeo, Bristol, Maserati and, of course, Ferrari.

Not that Feeley's work was in any way a clone of Touring's; there was a greater simplicity about it and a marked absence of embellishment except around the early radiator grilles. The styling was characterised by a smoothness of converging lines that draws the eye to the rear, where one would normally find a boot. The DB2, however, merely employed a small hatch for the spare wheel, so that all luggage had to be stuffed behind the seats, which would make for some interesting accidents; however pretty, the DB2 would not be a chiropractor's favourite. This was a lack that would be addressed in a groundbreaking way with the next Aston Martin road car, but one with which less athletic owners would have some problems.

Indeed, although Feeley's work was very much up to the moment in terms of general continental and American trends, the DB2 was a car that also possessed many styling features that were imitated back in Italy; the Fiat 8V, for example, has a distinct DB2 look about the rear quarters, but the bluff front end of the Aston, a theme that would persist through the next several models, could seldom be mistaken for anything else.

Another feature that set the Aston Martin apart from its Italian contemporaries was its sheer build

View of the DB2 engine. This first iteration of the Watson-Bentley engine has a reputation for fragility.

A DB2 engine showing Weber carburettors installed. This engine was originally fitted to a DB3S racing car.

The likelihood of body parts being exactly transferable between cars is still remote, however, as bodies were built to individual chassis. Indeed, they still are. It is a consistent theme of Aston Martin bodywork that it is more or less faultless in its execution, and that trend started here. However, Astons are still hand-made, so exact symmetry remains rare, and is probably coincidental.

The overall package, whatever reservations one has about the engine, is an attractive one and the DB2 proved relatively trouble-free. The sheer simplicity of the chassis layout and the robust (if noisy) reliability of the Salisbury axle, the David Brown transmission, and the Girling brakes offer a long life. The electrical equipment, however, is mainly by Lucas, and is not one of the model's strongest points.

quality. The English technique of rolling rather than beating out sheet alloy for bodies paid huge dividends in both quality and longevity. Whereas the Italian manner of literally bashing out the body shape, one worker per side, and zipping the two halves together afterwards, often produced observable asymmetry, the method used to make the DB2, one panel at a time, had the advantage of greater consistency as well as the presence of little or no body filler.

Looking at the DB2 chassis in detail, it is a shortened version of Claude Hill's 1939 Atom work as seen on the DB1, and is of mainly square tube construction with a wheelbase of 8ft 3in (2.5m). Bulkheads and wheel arches are from fabricated sheet steel and the central body frame is of Z-section steel reinforced by narrow-gauge tubing. It is reminiscent of the Superleggera school of design, but

In a corner of the works two DB2 chassis are prepared for the 1949 Le Mans race.

Reg Parnell with a DB2 competition car.

that is a later association; it is heavier, a beefy piece of engineering.

The suspension, particularly when compared with the contemporary Italian offerings, is both supple and sophisticated, with coil springs all round. Trailing links are used at the front, while at the back parallel arms, supported by a Panhard rod, locate the live axle. As a result, the handling of a DB2 is of a higher order than many of its contemporary rivals, and one of its strongest points.

The body, of 18 standard wire gauge aluminium alloy, is clenched around the steel framework; the bonnet is a one-piece alloy unit that hinges at the nose and opens through 45°. The two-piece windscreen is of flat glass with a slight rake. The rear screen is small and laterally curved over the radius of the rear roof; it sits high, and rear visibility is consequently poor, a feature exacerbated by the huge ground clearance. You will not see the Lamborghini behind you.

Early 1950 cars have a three-piece radiator grille design that rather echoes the DB1; further, behind the front arches are a pair of washboard-

like vents that happily disappeared on later cars. The bumpers are merely rubbing strips of double-radiused alloy; they are fixed tight to the front and rear and, on certain earlier cars, along the length of the sills around the whole car.

Inside, the simplicity continues; there are two flat leather-covered seats, which offer little in the way of support, but some adjustment fore and aft is possible. The door trims are similarly leather-covered and the carpet is wool Wilton. The dashboard is a simple wooden panel containing, from left to right, a circular ignition/switch unit, a speedometer with built-in clock, a four-part combined oil pressure gauge, ammeter, water thermometer and fuel gauge, and a tachometer.

Electrical equipment is all British: Smiths instruments, Lucas ancillaries and an SU fuel pump. The wipers are, typical of the time, dismal, and the SU pump can fail. In my view it is best replaced, or at least augmented.

The engine is a six-cylinder in-line, iron-blocked twin overhead camshaft unit, of 78mm bore and 90mm stroke, displacing 2,580cc. The initial compression ratio was a low 6.5:1, reflecting the low quality of pool

Tadek Marek

Marek's engineering background was rather narrower than that of Harold Beach. He joined Aston Martin in 1954 from Austin, where he had worked on military powerplants. His first job was to redesign the offset 3-litre engine used in the DB2/4 series, to produce the DBA family. In this he was assisted by Beach, and the result was the most powerful version of it, the DBC.

By 1955 he had started work on its successor, Project 186, the DB4 engine. Initially of 3,670cc capacity, it was taken out to nearly 4 litres for racing, which became its standard specification after DB4 production finished in 1963, by which time Marek was already working on the V8 intended for the DBS. DP 186 had its teething problems, but it became one of the greats.

The Callaway-tuned V8 in current use is thus a direct descendant of the original engine started in 1962, the main difference being its four-valve layout. Marek's work has stood the test of time very well, and the engine, when compared to its contemporaries, whether V12s from Italy or V8s from America or Germany, is clearly in a class of its own. Marek died in 1985.

A line-up of DB2 racers.

petrol available at the car's inception. There are two valves per cylinder, at 60° to each other, and power output was quoted at 105bhp at 5,000rpm. From January 1951 a 'Vantage' tune was offered, which consisted of some top-end modifications: a higher compression ratio, of 8.16:1, and larger SU carburettors, producing 125bhp at 5,000rpm. The engine connects to the transmission via a 9-inch Borg & Beck single dry-plate clutch.

The gearbox is a David Brown unit, with four forward speeds and a Porsche-designed synchromesh on all gears. There is a choice of internal ratios on second and third gears, moving them closer together. First and top are unchanged, however, whether the gearbox is close-ratio or not.

The rear axle is a Salisbury hypoid type with a choice of final drives: 3:77:1 was standard, but options included 3.5:1, 3.67:1 and 4.1:1. With standard gearing on 6.00 x 16-inch tyres, the car will cruise at 21.4mph per 1,000rpm in top gear. No overdrive was offered at the time, but some cars will be found with it retrofitted; it is a good idea, provided that the speedometer cable has been changed to match the final drive ratio, otherwise things get very confusing.

A DB2 was very nearly my first Aston Martin. In 1982 I had seen an advertisement offering one for sale from a garage tucked away in the warren of mews that surround South Kensington. It was, I think, about £1,200. Given the inflationary expectations that were still part of my soul, it did not seem too bad against the £400 or so that could have secured me one of Mr Goldstone's. Having bought it on the phone, when I turned up with the money I was mortified to see its shapely tail disappearing around the corner, driven (inexpertly, I will always think) by its proud new owner. Ah, the motor trade. It was a nice one, actually, with Webers and a 'competition history'. Allegedly. But then they all seemed to be either former Le Mans racers or former Peter Sellers cars then. I bought a DB4 instead, for rather less money. It needed only an engine.

It is unlikely that any DB2 is going to be exactly as original in the performance stakes. Very few, if any, will have survived in a pure unadulterated state, and, given that this book serves as an introduction to these cars, a few points are worth making.

The progress made in power assistance, sound insulation and suspension materials since 1949 has been huge, and bear in mind that this car has a separate chassis, not to

mention that the body clings to the frame more or less via its own tension rather than by any high-tech type of metal closure.

Start the engine and discover how noisy these cars are; it is not obtrusive as such, but you can certainly hear it working. The clutch is relatively heavy, the steering more so, with that curious dead feel at low speed, a function of the worm-and-roller steering box. It works well, however, particularly as the car gets under way. Given the noise it makes, it feels faster than it really is. Quoted acceleration figures suggest 0–60 in about 11 seconds and a maximum of 117mph, which was very similar to the Jaguar XK120. Bear in mind that testers were (and are) no respecters of mechanical integrity; try to match those figures in an unmodified DB2 today, particularly if it is yours, and things could get expensive. However, for its time it is a fast car, and as you

A DB2 competition car interior.

approach maximum legal speeds it feels comfortable with them and cruises happily at 70–80mph. The transmission is first-rate, with a precise notchy shift.

The brakes can squeal, judder and fade, even if fitted with the optional alloy Alfin drums; this is true of most of the DB2 generation, as the brakes are not really up to the performance. The swept area is a mere 152sq in, so a hefty shove is needed to decelerate from motorway speed. Also, the DB2 can be awkward in nose-to-tail traffic, not because people stare, but because driver confidence drops. Don't forget that there are no real bumpers.

Into a corner, handling is relatively neutral. The tail can be made to move out more or less at will and a workmanlike drift can be set up and managed; not that it is really necessary, as the road-holding is a revelation, even to a driver spoiled by modern front-wheel-drive hot hatchbacks. If the tail does go, however, it is easily caught. Of course, such antics are more properly carried out on a track. It is a recurring

feature of Aston Martins that, as they are relatively heavy for their power output and their running gear owes a lot to racing development, they can be driven safely but selfishly on the road, if that is your preference. All very enjoyable, but not everyone would agree.

The best way to enjoy a DB2, like most of its cousins, is on a decent secondary road. The performance in the indirect gears, particularly third, endows the car with a character that simply cannot be found today. Only when driving on really bad surfaces does the dated nature of the flexible chassis reveal itself in scuttle shake and a distinct sense of wobble from the huge bonnet.

In short, the DB2, considering the circumstances in which it was developed – after the merger of two struggling firms, some hard decisions resulting in the departure of key staff, and a fiercely competitive market – was a startling success. It was not the best car of its line, as things turned out, but it was certainly the purest and the prettiest, and the closest in concept to what Claude Hill had originally designed.

DB2s at speed.

Buying Hints

These cars are relatively scarce; only 409 were made in total, so unless there is a dire economic crisis under way, it is usually something of a seller's market, unless of course there is something wrong with the car. Many Astons do get sold under duress, but mainly because of the daunting cost of repairing them, which is a function not of particularly high labour costs on the part of the specialists, but because some of the work is extremely time-consuming and some of the spares can be risibly expensive.

All the usual rules of car-buying apply, but happily Aston DB2s and their derivatives are actually quite simple and much is visible.

1. After ensuring that the chassis is straight, by checking the height at all four corners and looking closely at door gaps, open the vast bonnet and check its underside for inexpert repair. A bodge here could indicate a bodge elsewhere. To the front you will see the transverse oil-filled tube that carries the torsion bar; look at it closely for accident damage and/or leaks, as it will be hard to replace.

2. The front of the chassis should also be inspected closely, particularly the bonnet hinges – if they are heavily packed or shimmed, check that the shimming is even and consistent; asymmetry here could suggest crash damage.

3. The bodywork should be straight and even with no discernible ripples. In profile, the front edge of the door, where it meets the rear edge of the bonnet, should be an even straight line. The bottom edge of the door should line up with the bottom edge of the bonnet; where the two lines cross there should be four equal 90° angles. If there are not, check that the bonnet locking bar under the dash is fully home. If it is,

check the front of the car very carefully indeed for accident damage.

4. When inspecting the engine, forget what it looks like – that is neither here nor there. Is the oil clean? Remove both the radiator and oil filler caps and check whether the oil and water are mixing. If they are it suggests a head gasket problem. There are many tales of engine rebuilds being carried out by inexpert engineers who have misjudged the clearance by which the cylinder liners sit proud of the block; unless the clearance is exact, the gasket will not seal properly and will start leaking. Gaskets also leak for other reasons, of course, mainly to do with overheating; a defunct water pump is not unheard of, for example. If the engine has been rebuilt recently, then the dreaded gasket syndrome will necessitate full investigation.

5. Another problem with these units is their propensity to crack the engine block. The signs of repair are always evident, despite the fact that they are often lacquered bright red. The indicators, a line of weld or traces of 'stitching', suggest that something major has happened in the past, which is all the more reason to check very carefully for emulsified oil in the water. If the block has gone, it almost certainly devalues the car, for although replacements are now available, they are by no means cheap, as well as requiring building up.

The block weakness stems from two inherent design weaknesses, which exacerbate each other: the most obvious is the thinness of the metal between the water conduits and the block itself, the other being the loadings imposed upon the bottom end due first to the unique way in which the crank and its bearings are built up, and second to the loadings imposed upon the liners. It all makes for potential

difficulties when the engine ages and internal corrosion weakens the water jacket.

6. Start the engine. Listen for the usual 'diesel' noises that suggest worn bearings and piston slap, and check the oil pressure. When cold it should be high, as much as 85psi; when at normal temperature, the engine should offer at least 60psi at 4,000rpm. If it is off the clock, however, be suspicious. The readings should not be volatile: up quickly, down more slowly.

7. A word about engine bays. An engine that is immaculate in appearance but which fails to deliver the goods in terms of oil pressure, compression or power is not worth paying a premium for. It is merely sculpture.

My favourite motor trade character, the obviously inbred but determinedly cheery psychopath with the funny haircut, an enviable line in bovine effluent and apparently only a cellular telephone number, may consider the few quid invested in 'detailing' the engine bay a useful alternative to actually making the wretched thing run correctly, even if he knows how to do it. He will possibly have learned this trick as a Triumph Stag specialist. Lovely presentation, but couldn't pull your socks up.

Likewise, he will helpfully point out the small rectangular tear in the headlining when you are more concerned about the dismally revealing roux that coats the inside of the radiator cap. Mind your eye with these people. All these cars are old, comebacks are few, and remedial work is, by any standards, expensive. If his parting comment as you drive away is, 'And if it turns out to have been the spare car for Le Mans, then good luck to you, mate', assume that he knows that it was not.

Aston Martin DB2/4

It was clear, quite early into the life of the DB2, that it was not very roomy. The lack of a boot, as well as the uncompromising two-seater cabin, placed great restrictions on the uses to which it could be put. To be sure, it had performed well in competition, but was not a customer racer; although well-trimmed, it was noisy and inconvenient for a road car. It carried very little luggage.

Time and time again, however, the development of a decent two-seater into a user-friendly 2+2 is fraught with difficulty, and very few have done it. Jaguar's later attempt with the E-Type is a good example of how

not to, although Lotus, it must be said, made a fair fist of it with the larger Elan.

In Aston Martin's case, they tried to do everything at once. The provision of both folding rear seats and a liftback tailgate was, on the face of it, too much. Innovative though the tailgate was, it was bulbous; a solution was to add proper bumpers fore and aft to visually lengthen the car by 7 inches while maintaining the same wheelbase. Two further changes were to raise the headlights by 2 inches and substitute a single-piece windscreen for the twin flat glass screens of the DB2. Some of the lithe aggression of the DB2 was

The DB2/4 lost some of the proportions of its predecessor, but not critically so. The hatchback tail is just as useful for shopping as it is for golf-clubs.

The front aspect of the 2/4 shows the more substantial bumpers. Visually they lengthen the car and make the more rounded rear end less obvious. The screen is no longer split.

Aston Martin DB2/4
October 1953–October 1955

VB6/J ENGINE:
(Standard after VB6/B until end of production)
As VB6/E except:
Bore x stroke	83 x 90mm
Capacity	2992cc
Power	140bhp at 5,000rpm

TRANSMISSION:
Four-speed manual David Brown gearbox with synchromesh on all gears
Final drive   3.77:1 (standard); 3.5:1, 3.67:1 and 4.1:1 optional

SUSPENSION:
Coil springs all round.
Front: Trailing links
Back: Live rear axle with parallel arms supported by a Panhard rod
Steering: Worm and roller

BRAKES:	12-inch drums
WHEELS:	6.00 x 16-inch
BODYWORK:	Separate steel body and chassis
LENGTH:	14ft 1½in (4.3m)
WIDTH:	5ft 5in (1.65m)
WHEELBASE:	8ft 3in (2.51m)
HEIGHT:	4ft 5½in (1.36m)
WEIGHT (dry):	23.2cwt (1,180kg)
MAX SPEED: 0–60mph (97kph)	117mph (188kph) c11 seconds
PRICE NEW:	£2,600

PRODUCTION FIGURES:
565, including at least 73 dropheads
Chassis numbers: LML/501 to LML/1065

unavoidably lost by these changes, but by and large the operation was a success; the DB2 was transformed into a car in which the driver could transport golf clubs, fishing rods, or enough luggage for a long trip. The DB2 chassis was more or less left intact, save some spatial adjustments

The tiny, bidet size seats were over the rear axle...

at the rear and a smaller fuel tank. All in all, the dry weight of the car increased by 200lb (91kg).

The new car's body was again manufactured under subcontract by Mulliner of Birmingham; a little further south, the Newport Pagnell firm of Tickford was tooling up for Lagonda production. Quite soon, Tickford would be bought by Brown and all Aston Martin and Lagonda

A 2/4 outside the AML works at Newport Pagnell. They were never built there, of course.

The same rear lamps are used on the DB2 and the 2/4.

coachwork would be built there. Indeed, ultimately the whole firm would move to Newport Pagnell, but not during the life of these cars.

In order to hold parity with the DB2 in terms of performance, the Vantage tune of the old model, which delivered 125bhp, was used as the standard tune for the DB2/4, and a choice of gear and axle ratios similar to the DB2 was offered to produce a package that reduced driver pleasure not at all.

There was no pleasure for the rear passengers, however. The tiny, bidet-sized seats were placed almost over the rear axle and headroom was modest. However, the point of the DB2/4 was not that it was in any way a family car, merely that occasional lifts could be given and luggage carried.

But there was no point in standing still. Willie Watson had been busy redesigning certain elements of the LB6 engine in order to take it out to 2.9 litres. For reasons of economy, in order to use the same basic castings, the bores were increased by 5mm to 83mm and offset slightly, but in pairs.

This meant of course that the connecting rods were also offset (which would cause some problems later), but the resultant redesign took the quoted power up to a useful 140bhp at 5,000rpm. These engines had been tried out on the DB3 racer and would find their way into the DB3S (see the next chapter).

The VB6/E Vantage tune of the DB2 became the standard offering of the DB2/4 in 2.6-litre form until the new engine (VB6/J) was introduced in the summer of 1954, so no particular Vantage tune was offered for this model.

Right top:
The DB2/4 hatchback.

Right bottom:
The DB2/4 drophead.

The DB3, DB3S
and Lagonda V12

The story of the racing Aston Martins is a long and complicated one, and as such is outside the scope of this book. Nonetheless, due to the important role they played, both in strict competition terms and in assisting the development of the road cars, they more than deserve to be included.

At the Tourist Trophy race at Dundrod, Ulster, on 15 September 1951, a new Aston Martin appeared.

It was rather late, as it had been hoped that the car would be ready in time for the Le Mans race that June. The car was the DB3, and it was the fruit of a year's labour on the part of the Feltham works under the direction of a new Chief Engineer, Dr Robert Eberan von Eberhorst, and he was a very careful man indeed.

Von Eberhorst had been rescued from virtual wage slavery by David Brown; he had been working for the ERA company, rump of the great pre-war

One of five DBR1s made: the cars started in 16 races and scored eight victories as well as scooping the World Sports Car Championship.

voiturette manufacturer, which was now owned by Leslie Johnson, who had co-driven the 1948 Spa race with Horsfall. Von Eberhorst, who for a while was also technically (or at least legally) owned by Johnson, had been instrumental in designing the mighty pre-war Auto-Union racing cars, and while he never did any good with ERA, chiefly because he was the only tangible asset of the firm, Aston Martin had high hopes of him. His best work in Britain thus far had been the Jowett Jupiter chassis, which was a good start.

Slowly, meticulously, to the drumming of impatient fingers, he created a robust ladder-framed chassis (in other words two hefty tubes) suspended by torsion bars, with inboard rear brakes and a Panhard rod holding the de Dion axle in place at the rear. The engine, effectively a DB2 Vantage unit of 2.6-litre capacity, was fitted with three 36mm Weber carburettors and, with an 8.16:1 compression, produced a lusty 140bhp. Transmission was via a five-speed S527 David Brown gearbox. The bodywork was simple enough and clearly a development of what a stripped-out DB2 barchetta might look like.

However, the DB3 was to be a disappointment, although it served well as a test bed for a handful of developments that would play their role later. Aston Martin campaigned four of them as team cars, the rest being sold to customers.

The VB6 engine that powered the DB3 was clearly going to struggle against larger-engined opposition. Given that the car, while using essentially a similar engine to the DB2 that had proved it could endure long races, had only achieved a few class wins, the prospects were gloomy. Basically the car was too heavy. It stopped well, but rather too often of its own accord.

Over the winter of 1952/3, Willie Watson, neatly circumventing von

Eberhorst to whom he reported, approached (for which read 'sidled up to') John Wyer with some ideas on improving the car, and Wyer, frustrated by the pace of Eberhorst's work, assented. Watson had scored some points by increasing the capacity of the 2.6-litre engine, and locked himself away to emerge in the spring of 1953 with a modified design. It was basically a slimmer, lighter DB3 chassis, to be clothed in some of Frank Feeley's best work. Von Eberhorst, ever the gent, said nothing.

The DB3S is, without doubt, one of the prettiest cars ever made. With

Virtually every V12 engine was a prototype, with the huge one-off costs associated with that

Watson's modifications (more of a redesign, really), the new car was 170lb (77kg) lighter than the DB3, which gave its rather overworked engine more of a chance. Other modifications included a four-speed gearbox, a lighter, spiral-bevel differential, and a sliding link to replace the Panhard rod.

The engine fitted was Watson's 2,922cc modification of the original Bentley/Watson design, as tried out on the DB3, and a version of which would power the DB2/4. The extra capacity was released by a curious method of offsetting the connecting rods in order to compensate for the fact that the six cylinders were now paired, which was the only way available of increasing their bore. This would put strain on the little-ends of the conrods more than once;

John Wyer

David Brown first set eyes on Wyer at the Spa 24-hour race in 1948; Wyer's pit management of Dudley Folland's privately entered pre-war Aston Martin impressed him deeply. Wyer joined Aston Martin in 1950 as Competitions Manager, and was appointed General Manager in 1956. Reg Parnell succeeded him on the racing side.

Wyer put his stamp very firmly on the competition department of Aston Martin. He was, according to those who knew him, a strict disciplinarian, although all the evidence suggests that in this he always fought a losing battle, at least off the track, as the antics of the Aston team became infamous.

Despite the fact that he lived to be 80 years old, he never enjoyed good health and upon retiring from racing after running Ford GT40s, Ford Mirages and Porsches in World Championship events, went to live in Arizona, where the clear desert air helped his lungs.

He will go down in racing lore as one of the finest managers to grace a pit lane, and there is no doubt that without his attention to detail Aston Martin would have fared much worse than it did. He died in April 1989.

A DB3 racer, photographed at Wiscombe Park hillclimb.

in fact, two DB3s powered by this engine had broken their conrods at the 1952 Monaco sports car race.

Despite this engineering inexactitude, the DB3S was to have a promising 1953, winning the British Empire Trophy in June. Further wins at Silverstone, Charterhall, Goodwood and Dundrod served notice that the elegant little car was, since its makeover, a serious contender.

In 1954 all that was reversed with a disastrous season, and Watson, excellent though his reworking of the DB3's chassis had been, easily made up for it with the costly blunder of the Lagonda V12 racing project. Despite the fact that he was nominally reporting to von Eberhorst as Chief Engineer, Watson was a slightly wilful fellow and, having been the chief designer on the LB6 engine, which certainly worked (whatever reservations one has about it), he decided to evolve the principle into a huge 4¼-litre Lagonda V12 racing engine. This was a subject close to David Brown's heart, as he wanted a big-bore racing unit with which he could challenge Ferrari. The LB6, with its iron block, had its shortcomings already, but Watson's decision to use alloy for both crankcase and bearing supports for the new V12 was not his best idea.

Before this fatal flaw was discovered, the DB3S chassis was stretched to accommodate the new engine and the car was built up. It was clear when it was fired up that the alloy crankcase was expanding as fast as the alloy 'doughnuts' that held the seven main bearings in place. It was a race that could have no winner. The result was that the bearing clearances just grew, and it was hard to hold oil pressure, which on a racing engine is critical. The project was scrapped

after a few forays, but the chassis would be back.

As you can imagine, this was all vastly expensive. Virtually every V12 engine was a prototype, with the huge one-off costs associated with that. It was this expenditure that led to the famously amusing encounter between Reg Parnell, the Aston Martin racing manager, and Brian Lister at the end of the 1957 season. Aston Martin had

Small and agile, the DB3S could race larger adversaries with a very good chance of success

enjoyed a good European season, but domestically they had only once beaten the Lister, which was Jaguar-powered. Parnell asked his adversary how much his season's racing had cost. Lister replied, 'Oh, about £5,000 or so', at which Parnell nearly blew a gasket – such a budget might pay for one cylinder head at Feltham.

Meanwhile the DB3S soldiered on with honours until the end of 1956, at which time it was replaced by the DBR1. In all 31 were built, in four different body styles. They continued to race in private hands after the factory moved on to other things, and indeed still do.

What made the DB3S an important car, if that is the word, was its ability to compete with more powerful adversaries with a good chance of success. It was small and agile and, while it was not underpowered in road car terms, it was in terms of competition, particularly when put up against the meatier Ferraris and Maseratis. But it handled. It was

possibly one of the most balanced cars ever to come out of Aston Martin.

Its successor, the DBR1, was almost entirely the work of Ted Cutting. This was the car that would finally deliver victory at Le Mans and in the World Sports Car Championship in 1959. Cutting started work on it in June of 1955 and it was ready for the 1956 Le Mans race, where it lasted a respectable 20 hours. Cutting was to finally achieve with this car his long-held objective of redesigning the bottom end of the racing engine with plain bearings, which he did in 1956. The development of the RB6 engine, the racing variant of the LB6, is inextricably linked to Cutting, among others, and is remarkable for the way in which motorcycle technology was applied. Whereas G. A. Vandervell went to Norton motorcycles for the inspiration for his Vanwall engine, Cutting and his team went to AJS; with their help they were able to develop the RB6 engine, using noisy gear-driven cams, to spin up to 6,500rpm and produce nearly 100bhp per litre, something of a Holy Grail at the time. In this form, fitted to the DBR1, the engine, along with Roy Salvadori, provided the long-sought-after victory at Le Mans in 1959.

Aston Martin DB2/4 Mark II

The temptation to fiddle with the aesthetics of the DB2/4 proved too much to resist, and the acquisition of the Tickford coachbuilding concern, based at Newport Pagnell, offered a chance to experiment. Tickford had an enviable tradition in coachbuilding circles; established as Salmon's in 1820, they had been building motor bodies since 1907 and gained a following with their Tickford drophead coachwork for road cars, the best known being on the MG chassis. The company changed its name from Salmon to Tickford in 1940 and David Brown bought it in 1953. Since the firm's post-war revival it had been the main bodywork contractor for the Lagonda range, and Brown was their biggest customer.

The Tickford designers quickly realised that the bonnet of the DB2/4 was simply too big and floppy. By separating the side panels and mounting them separately, a great deal of shake was removed. It was a distinct improvement. Not so the rest of the car. It was felt that the 2/4 was cramped, and indeed it was, particularly in the back. The solution, to raise the roofline by 1½ inches, was not a complete visual disaster, but the hasty addition of strips of bright metal around the roofline and new bonnet line probably was.

A DB2/4 Mark II. This Tickford-built car was considered by some to be over-decorated.

Tickford did, however, create a marvellous-looking fixed-head coupé on this chassis, of which around 35 were built. They followed the roofline of the two dozen dropheads also produced, and remain, despite their clear resemblance to the

Tickford did create a handsome fixed-head coupé on this chassis

contemporary Lagonda 3 litre, supremely elegant cars. Unfortunately, they are also extremely sought after. In fact, this version of the DB2/4 Mark II remains possibly the most coveted of the DB2 series, apart from the team cars and the three extravagant 'spyders' built by Touring of Milan, the first fruit of an association that was to last ten years.

This car is therefore merely a re-styled DB2/4. It is unlikely that it will ever go down in history as one of the greats, and our cheery psychopath will always overprice it, but if you seek a 2/4 this will be as cheap a way to own one as you will get. They are, however, rare. This has nothing to do with demand, but rather supply. The car was greeted politely at the 1955 Motor Show, but records reveal that only 199 were made, of which only about 135 were 'ordinary' saloons.

As the pundits say, when you are buying a 'pre-owned' car you will handicap yourself if you determine on a particular colour, and so it is with seeking out a 2/4. The Mark II is a sound car and the styling details can be looked at as merely quaint or unfortunate; they do not detract from the fact that 1950s sports saloons of this quality are, of themselves, rare things, and when all is said and done this is an Aston Martin. I have seen one car that has been 'cleansed' of the rather nasty exterior trim, and I have to say that it looked quite

Aston Martin DB2/4 Mark II
October 1955–August 1957

ENGINE (Standard VB6/J):
In-line six-cylinder, iron-block

Bore x stroke	83 x 90mm
Capacity	2992cc
Valves	Twin ohc
Compression ratio	8.16:1
Carburettors	Two 1.75in SUs
Power	140bhp at 5,000rpm

TRANSMISSION:
Four-speed manual David Brown gearbox with synchromesh on all gears
Final drive   3.77:1 (standard); 3.5:1, 3.67:1 and 4.1:1 optional

SUSPENSION:
Coil springs all round.
Front: Trailing links
Back: Live rear axle with parallel arms supported by a Panhard rod
Steering: Worm and roller

BRAKES:	12-inch drums
WHEELS:	6.00 x 16-inch
BODYWORK:	Separate steel body and chassis

LENGTH:	14ft 3½in (4.36m)
WIDTH:	5ft 5in (1.65m)
WHEELBASE:	8ft 3in (2.51m)
HEIGHT:	4ft 6¼in (1.38m)
WEIGHT (dry):	24.1cwt (1,226kg)
MAX SPEED:	117mph (188kph)
0–60mph (97kph)	c11 seconds
PRICE NEW:	£2,700

VB6/J L ENGINE (Special Series):
As VB6/J except:

Compression ratio	8.6:1
Carburettors	Two 1.75in SUs (three 40mm Weber DCOs optional)
Power	165bhp at 5,000rpm

PRODUCTION FIGURES:
199, including at least 24 dropheads, 34 coupés and 2 Touring 'spyders'
Chassis numbers: AM300/1101 to AM300/1299

fetching, for underneath the superficial flash the car's proportions are pleasing. Better, it has a proper cad's handbrake, which can confuse the psychopath.

It boasts a zippy engine, though. The standard offering, the VB6, was carried over from the first DB2/4 and produced the same 140bhp, but there was a Special Series alternative that had bigger valves and hairier cams, delivering 165bhp. The optional addition of triple 40mm Weber DCO carburettors improved top-end breathing, albeit at the cost of lumpy tickover (it was ever thus), so in 'top spec' this is really rather a fast car, if tiresome in traffic.

Aston Martin
DB Mark III

'James Bond flung the DB III through the last mile of straight and did a racing change down into third and then into second for the short hill before the inevitable traffic crawl through Rochester. Leashed in by the velvet claw of the front discs, the engine muttered its protest with a mild back-popple from the twin exhausts.'

Some extras here for the Aston Martin buff, and not all of them from Q branch either. The introduction of front disc brakes was to improve the DB2 series dramatically, but not as much as the extensively revised engine found on the DB Mark III. (It is not, actually, called a DBIII; the DB3 was the racer designed by von Eberhorst.)

The DB Mark III: note the DB3S-style grille. Embellishment aside, the body was basically that of the Mark II. Originally export only, the car made a name for itself as the first James Bond Aston, in *Goldfinger*.

The shortcomings of the original LB6 engine were almost a thing of the past by the time Tadek Marek and the ubiquitous Harold Beach had finished with it; the bottom end of the engine was still constructed in the same strange way, but there were other considerable improvements that went a long way toward compensating for the eccentricity of the layout. The most obvious changes to the car, however, were external.

The cluttered lines of the Mark II were banished into the outer darkness and the snout of the car was modified to reflect the appearance of the racing machines. It was a very tidy design, and was echoed inside with the instrument binnacle following the shape of the nose intake; hitherto the

The Mark III was the best road Aston Martin yet

dashboard of an Aston Martin could well have been from a First World War aircraft.

The rear wing line shape was retained, but new vertical, long and narrow tail lamps were installed (which can also be seen on the Alvis TD-TF series). It seems that some early cars used the old Mark II lights, but records are inexact as to how many there were to this configuration.

But it was in the engine room that the Mark III really shone. The LB6 engine now had a new block casting and was renamed as the DBA series. The block was stiffer, as was the crank, and the breathing was much improved, even in standard form.

The net result was that standard power output went up to 160bhp, with the most exotic option offering a claimed 214bhp. Even if you believe these figures (and many do not), the

Aston Martin DB Mark III
March 1957–July 1959

ENGINE (Standard DBA):
In-line six-cylinder, iron-block

Bore x stroke	83 x 90mm
Capacity	2922cc
Valves	Twin ohc
Compression ratio	8.16:1
Carburettors	Two 1.5in SUs
Power	162bhp at 5,500rpm

TRANSMISSION:
Four-speed manual David Brown gearbox with synchromesh on all gears
Final drive   3.77:1 (standard); 3.5:1, 3.67:1 and 4.1:1 optional

SUSPENSION:
Coil springs all round.
Front: Trailing links
Back: Live rear axle with parallel arms supported by a Panhard rod
Steering: Worm and roller

BRAKES:	Discs at front, drums at rear
WHEELS:	6.00 x 16-inch
BODYWORK:	Separate steel body and chassis
LENGTH:	14ft 3½in (4.36m)
WIDTH:	5ft 5in (1.65m)
WHEELBASE:	8ft 3in (2.51m)
HEIGHT:	4ft 6½in (1.38m)
WEIGHT (dry):	25cwt (1,271kg)
MAX SPEED:	117mph (188kph)
0–60mph (97kph)	c11 seconds
PRICE NEW:	£3,000

DBB ENGINE (optional):
As DBA except:

Compression ratio	8.6:1
Carburettors	Three 35mm Webers
Power	195bhp at 5,500rpm

DBC ENGINE (optional):
As DBA except:

Compression ratio	9.1:1
Carburettors	Three 45mm Webers
Power	214bhp at 5,500rpm

DBD ENGINE (optional):
As DBA except:

Compression ratio	8.6:1
Carburettors	Two/three 1.5in SUs
Power	180bhp at 5,500rpm

PRODUCTION FIGURES:
551, including 84 dropheads coupés and 5 fixed-head coupés
Chassis numbers: AM300/3A/1300 to AM300/3/1850

The frontal treatment of the Mark III echoes the DB3S racing car.

Mark III was undeniably the best road Aston Martin yet. To drive one back to back with a standard 2.6-litre DB2/4 is to discover what motor racing, concentration, and a great deal of money can accomplish. Not only is the Mark III a fast and refined grand tourer, it is also undeniably elegant and clearly as good as, if not better than, a Jaguar XK140. Its optional disc brakes helped, but the grunt liberated by Beach and Marek from the original LB6 engine was easily equal to them; stopping the DB Mark III when in a hurry is not a task for the faint-hearted.

However, DB Mark IIIs are, like all these first-generation models, quite scarce, with total production of only 551 cars. Their manufacture overlapped with that of the Mark II for six months or so and, as the Mark III got into its stride as a benchmark by which other cars must be judged, it was triumphantly revealed that all the time there had been something rather special waiting in the wings – the DB4.

As we look back now at the nine years of the DB2 series of cars, they seem to be a startling achievement in many ways. The simple specifications were, at various stages, far ahead of their time: coil springs all round, for example, when most makers were using cart springs well into the 1960s; a quality of body manufacture that still sets standards today; an innovative hatchback design; a development flexibility unmatched by any other British manufacturer; and a simplicity of line (apart from the perhaps aberrant DB2/4 Mark II) that still delights today.

Further, the final incarnation of the LB6 engine, the DB series as fitted to the Mark III, really is a good piece of engineering and far better than the design from which it came; another example of how the application of lessons learned in endurance racing could have a direct and immediate effect on the engineering qualities of road cars.

It's fast and stable, handles well, stops smartly, and sounds good

Only a small-volume manufacturer could do this development with the same rapidity, aided, of course, by enthusiastic customers/racers with a taste for experimentation and expensive adventure. Aston Martin have always enjoyed this relationship with their clients and it was to bear fruit more than once in later years, providing an economical route to fast improvement.

Above all, the DB2 series demonstrates very well that a decent road car with competition potential does not need a huge fire-breathing engine: a sophisticated chassis, balance, poise and a forgiving nature are much more useful, and Lyndon Sims showed this rather well when he won the 1956 RAC Rally, in a very second-hand, four-year-old DB2.

The DB Mk III is probably the most

A DB Mark III anecdote

This is really a market story rather than a car one. I was in the market for a Mark III, having never owned one and regretting the lack somewhat. It was, I think, 1988 and I was strolling around what Alan Clark calls 'The Mews' on a Monday when I saw a decent-looking Mark III being unloaded in front of a well-known dealer. Because it was a bright day I could see that the car was unusually straight and also that it was my favourite colour, a gunmetal grey. Close up, the trim looked a little home-made, but Feltham Astons are simplicity itself to re-trim so I wasn't worried about that.

Upon enquiry I gathered that it was 'just in' from South Africa and was for sale. We agreed the price – £34,000 as I recollect – after a spin around Hyde Park, which revealed that the clutch was shot, the engine OK and the re-trim courtesy of some endangered species of antelope, carried out by another endangered species, a white Zimbabwe farmer, who had owned the car for 20-odd years. The tyres were of a make unknown to me, so I asked if a new clutch, new Dunlops and an oil service could be carried out speedily enough for me to pick up the car, with MoT, on Friday. 'No problemo, squire,' or words to that effect. I gave them a cheque as a deposit for both the work and the car, and departed.

So imagine my surprise when I arrived back at the establishment on Friday, negotiable cashier's draft in hand, to find 'my' car, looking splendid I must say, parked outside with a small crowd around it. I delivered the draft and was just about to sign the delivery slip when a small cough caught my ear. I know these small coughs – they invariably mean something. I was sure, for once in my life, that I had not issued a rubber cheque. I raised an eyebrow.

'Someone wants to buy your car.'

Now, I am a trader (although not of motor cars, as anyone who has sold me one will tell you), so I merely asked how much the punter was offering. There was some shuffling. '£47,000' (for which read at least £50,000). No wonder they were embarrassed. I looked at the car again, and, you will not be surprised to learn, it really was not as good as I had thought. I trousered the draft, accepted their cheque for the difference and went home. I felt justified in taking a taxi. Thirteen thousand pounds in four days (less expenses) was not too bad, and represented a sum of money that only a few years before would have bought me the best Mark III on the planet.

Lest anyone think that I feel clever about this, I must reassure them that I do not. That windfall profit did, I must confess, make up for some past follies, and I would manage to give most of it back over time, but the point of the story is really this. Whereas our cheery psychopath would have fobbed me off with a few thousand and a story, these guys were proper traders. It was clear that they were as startled as I was; they knew their market, they thought, and they knew me too. They were appalled that they had 'mispriced' the car to me to the extent that I could make as much out of it as they could (which is psychopath*ish*), but when chatting a few weeks later at one of the historic jollies, it was confided to me that this kind of hysteria was something quite new to them, and that if it can happen with price rises, then the reverse must also be true. The incident had made them nervous. The old car game was becoming a cross between pass the parcel and musical chairs. They were right. They are still in business. And I was (luckily) greedy. I'd still like to own a Mark III for more than four days, though.

Left top:
The rear of the Mark III has a distinctly Alfa Romeo look – but rather bigger.

Left bottom:
With the top raised, the profile is that of the coupé.

pleasing of the DB2 line. It is undeniably fast and stable, handles well, stops smartly and makes an evocative noise. And so it should. This is an engine that has derived its development purely from the track. The engine, aside from the eccentric architecture of the bottom end, has acquired much improvement from the racing cars, and it is as good an Aston with Watson/Bentley power as you can get.

So pleased were Aston Martin to have sorted out the LB6 engine that they offered a bewildering number of tuning options with the car. By now, having grown by only 400cc, its output had improved by 50 per cent in standard form to 160bhp. A DBC 'Competition' tune was available, which offered a rather hysterical 214bhp, provided by three large Webers and high compression, but

Despite its solid shape and extra weight, this car is nimble

hardly any were built. It is clear, however, that the dictum that has justified the comedic expense of motor racing over the years as research rather than fun was true in this case. The thrashing that the LB6 and its RB6 cousin received on the race track had, by 1957, paid huge dividends. It was an expensive car, in more ways than one.

Despite its solid appearance and extra weight, the DB Mk III is an agile car. The steering on the example I drove was well-balanced, but the cars often have a reputation for heaviness. Certainly, it is not exactly light at parking speeds.

One is conscious of the same general feeling about the car as about any of

its earlier relatives. The dashboard is much more up to date and functional – a version of it will be seen again on the DB4. Instrumentation is comprehensive, even by modern standards. Pedal pressure is comfortingly hard.

On the move, the car lightens up even more. Keeping an eye on the oil pressure while moving up through the gears, the improvements in porting and manifolding are clear. The throttle response is better on this engine, and the twin exhausts, minimally damped, boom pleasingly. There is still an element of shake from the huge bonnet, and a slight creak from the catch on the huge closing lever under the dash.

These DB Mark III rear lamps are also found on the Graber Alvis and the early DB4.

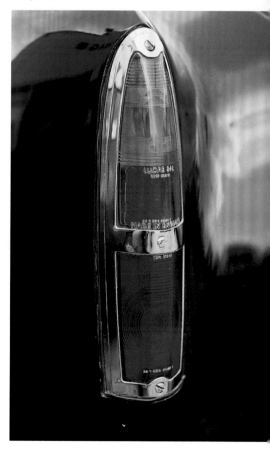

The cockpit of a Mark III drophead. Note the instrument binnacle, which apes the shape of the grille and was used up to the DB6.

It is fast, probably in XK150 territory and quicker (and infinitely more refined) than a Healey. The thin bucket seats are snug and the pedal location is good. Noise apart, it feels like a decent car for a long journey, the more so because it has overdrive. The gearchange is the robust David Brown unit, which we are now quite used to. It certainly has the edge over the Jaguar's Moss box, but then, to be fair, most things do.

But, of course, it should be a good car: at over £3,000 at introduction, it was Britain's costliest sports saloon. To think of it as an out-and-out sports car would be to misplace its purpose.

While it is long-legged, for urgent-running, and with the capacity for hustling along on lesser roads, it also

ambles nicely – a good all-rounder, and one of Aston Martin's nicest cars.

When I was jammed into the back seat of Mr Goldstone's car, inhaling that heady bouquet of mouldy carpet and hot oil, cut through with the sharp tang of spilt battery acid and the piscine top notes of dodgy wiring, I thought these cars were hugely fast. By modern standards, of course, they aren't. They are crude, noisy and primitive. But, by contrast, you actually do drive them. It is a selfish thing, but there really is a great pleasure in hustling, unnecessarily, one of these needlessly heavy 3-litre cars around a country road. The driver finds the car's limits quite quickly, but it is a generous, forgiving machine. Despite the fact that John Wyer always considered the Mark III something of an interim lash-up, it is a major success.

In conclusion, these first-generation Astons evoke the late 1940s. In their favour, they are strong structurally, and their mechanical components, if well sorted out, are reliable. They are as well built as any of their contemporaries and much better than most. As the DB2 series evolved it got better, and this is not always the case with British cars. The DB Mark III is the best of the line, whereas the XK150 is certainly not, and nor is the V12 E-Type.

The down side is really the same as for any other old car. They tend to be undergeared for motorway use and there is always the worry about engine condition. A properly rebuilt engine, using the lessons learned over the 50 years since the cars were conceived, will now perform in a manner much superior to when it was new. Oil has much to do with this, but the simple quality of work available now (as good as it has ever been), combined with the vast array of improved components that have been produced, should not put anyone off.

To drive, of course, these cars are not modern in any way; they have a separate chassis, primitive wipers, and noisy engines. To some they are magnificent, to others merely quaint. They handle well, and are respectably quick, but after a 2-hour drive you really know where you have been sitting.

The Mark III engine with triple SU carburettors.

Aston Martin DB4

In my view the DB4 is the definitive road-going post-war Aston Martin. Strong, fast and manoeuvrable, it personifies the marque in a way that no other type does. It was, however, a long time coming.

DP (Development Project) 114 was the putative successor to the DB2 series of cars and came into being on the drawing-board in May 1955. It used a perimeter frame chassis, wore a new Frank Feeley body and, thank heavens, never made it into production, remaining as a

development vehicle. Since the relationship between Aston Martin and the Touring company of Milan had borne elegant fruit with the 1956 DB2/4 'spyders', it was decided that Touring should be approached to design the next generation of cars. The imperatives of power and elegance, neither of which DP114 possessed in spadesful, ensured that it became merely a curiosity. It was replaced in late 1956 by DP184, a prototype of which was ready by September 1957.

The massive chassis frame of the DB4. Note the Superleggera tubes over which the thin alloy was laid.

Racing had taught Aston Martin much; the weaknesses of the Bentley/Watson school of engine design had given some pause for thought, and although the combined efforts of Willie Watson, Tadek Marek and Harold Beach had improved it somewhat, involving the re-invention of the block and taking the capacity out to nearly 3 litres, it had clearly reached the apogee of its development. Its bhp had, slightly breathlessly, been doubled. A new engine was called for. It was DP186.

Marek was a gifted engineer who had arrived at Feltham from Austin in 1954 as Chief Designer. At Austin he had worked mainly on heavy machinery, such as powerplants for Centurion tanks, and his brief was to design a new generation of engines. He was pleased to have the opportunity, and he was to pay out David Brown in the full coin of his mind. Twice, as it turned out.

The specification for the general layout of the new unit sounded familiar: six cylinders, twin overhead camshafts, iron block, about 3 litres. However, the lessons learned in

They knew that three litres was a benchmark for the carriage trade

attempting to increase the capacity of the LB6 unit, with its long stroke, led Marek to design the bottom end for a rather larger capacity than that, with proper plain bearings. This allowed him the luxury of no fewer than seven mains in which to carry the huge Laystall crankshaft. With an iron block, alloy head and two cams, the specification was starting to sound rather like a Coventry product. But Aston Martin had learned well from their racing. They also knew that 3 litres was a benchmark for the carriage trade: Alvis and Jaguar

Aston Martin DB4
Series 1
October 1958–February 1960

ENGINE:
In-line six-cylinder, alloy block and head

Bore x stroke	92 x 92mm
Capacity	3670cc
Valves	Twin ohc
Compression ratio	8.25:1
Carburettors	Two 2in SUs, single-plug ignition
Power	240bhp at 5,500rpm

TRANSMISSION:
David Brown four-speed manual gearbox with Salisbury hypoid final drive. Ratio 3.54:1. Other ratios optional.

SUSPENSION:
Coil springs all round.
Front: Transverse wishbones, ball-jointed kingpins, anti-roll bar, Armstrong telescopic dampers
Back: Live axle, trailing arms, Watt linkage, Armstrong lever-arm dampers
Steering: Rack and pinion

BRAKES:
Dunlop disc brakes all round. Lockheed vacuum servo

WHEELS:
16-inch Dunlop centre-lock wires; 16-inch Borrani optional extra. Tyres 6.00 x 16-inch crossply

BODYWORK:
Four-seater, two-door body, hand-made in magnesium aluminium alloy. Flat headlamps. All-steel platform chassis; body supported by Superleggera cage.

LENGTH:	14ft 9in (4.5m)
WIDTH:	5ft 6in (1.68m)
WHEELBASE:	8ft 2in (2.49m)
HEIGHT:	4ft 3½in (1.31m)
WEIGHT:	26.79cwt (1,362kg)
MAX SPEED:	c140mph (225kph) (depending on axle ratio)
PRICE NEW:	£4,000 at introduction

PRODUCTION FIGURES:

Series 1	149
Series 2	349
Series 3	164
Series 4	314
Series 5	134
Total	1,110, plus two prototypes, DP184/1 and 2

For detail changes through Series 2-5, see 'DB4 evolution' on page 50.

A very early DB4 with the lightweight bumpers, egg-box grille and earliest bonnet scoop that indicate the 'first of the first' series. The DB Mark III beside it illustrates the radical differences in design philosophy between the two cars.

produced 3-litre cars, and so normally did Ferrari, and it was between those marques that Aston Martin really saw their future. Alvises were civilised but sluggish; Ferraris were fast but crude; and Jaguars, when all was said and done, were mass-produced, albeit fast but arguably vulgar and a tad obvious. There was a niche. But a small one.

The targeted output of the basic engine before tuning was 180bhp, and in the proposed 3-litre guise it probably would have been, given what had been accomplished with the more highly tuned manifestations of the DBA–DBC series. However, the extra mass of the bottom end, liberated by sensible bearings – the use of conventional shells allowing a certain extravagance – permitted a larger capacity and, more important,

a shorter stroke. Now that petrol was becoming once more recognisable, the long engine strokes required to, as it were, crush the stuff, rather like some Third World maize-grinder, were becoming a thing of the past. The octane ratings of five-star fuel were in the area of 101. The engine could now work.

It was almost a coincidence that the first Marek engine had an alloy block; it transpired that the foundry that had been designated to cast it had no spare capacity for iron work (the mass market had bagged it), but did have space for alloy, so alloy it became, which caused its designer to flinch somewhat. This development was to cause headaches, particularly for Marek, who was insistent that his engine should not be raced, at least not initially.

With an alloy-blocked engine the difficulties caused by differing coefficients of expansion never really go away, and are only really addressed by retarding the speed with which the alloy heats up. If the block can remain cool enough for long enough, while the ferrous moving parts of the engine – crank, con-rods, liners and valve gear – heat up at their own pace, clearances between the two types of metal can be controlled and catastrophe averted. The problems encountered with the

internal plumbing of the LB6 engine, iron blocked though it was, arose from the use of the alloy 'doughnuts', which carried the crankshaft, and the grip, or lack of it, with which they held on to their cargo via the bearings.

This is, of course, why the oil capacity of a Marek-designed straight-six is so vast, and the pressure at which it flows is so high; the designer was justifiably nervous at the impact of endurance racing on an alloy-blocked engine. He was both right and wrong.

Jaguar were to encounter similar difficulties with alloy-blocked versions of their XK engine when they raced it in the 1960s, which is why they stuck to iron blocks for mass production (and racing) until oil technology caught up, which was only relatively recently. Arguably, the developments

This car, DB4 257R, was the works demonstrator loaned to *The Motor* for testing. It is a Series 2 model; note the revised bonnet scoop and heavier bumpers.

The DBR2

The chassis of the unloved and expensive Lagonda V12 racer had been lying about for too long at the Aston Martin racing shop. The engine had been abandoned by 1956, but it was felt that Willie Watson's chassis had further development merit, even if his engine did not. Tadek Marek had started work on his new straight-six the year before and it was felt (not by Marek) that the competition potential of DP186 could be explored by fitting it into the Lagonda frame. As the DBR1 was already under way, the new car would be the DBR2.

In fact, the cars used a variety of engines: for WSC endurance racing, the maximum permitted capacity was 3 litres, but for unlimited capacity events at the high club level, the DB4 engine could be usefully developed. It was with the new engine in 3.7-litre form that Aston Martin could take on the Jaguar XK, albeit now installed in Archie Scott Brown's awesome Lister Jaguar. Since the withdrawal of Jaguar from competition at the end of 1956, the Cambridge company had effectively flown Coventry's flag. Aston Martin had been struggling against the Lister all season, but finally they did it, at Silverstone in September 1957, when Salvadori managed to beat his favourite rival.

The DBR2, despite its appearance, is a radically different car from the DBR1. The body is similar to look at, but the chassis, very little modified from that of the Lagonda, was the work of Watson – the DBR1 was the work of Cutting.

The R. S. Williams Lightweight DB4s

To many, the development of these cars was anathema, while to others it was a simple question of economics. To some, it was what they had been waiting for. The escalating values of the DB4GT, of which few had been made, had for some time prompted various enthusiasts to improve their cars with competition in mind. A DB4GT was too rare and precious a car to risk on the track, and yet it remained the most competitive. A keen segment of the Aston Martin Owners' Club had for some time been tuning and improving their cars to the extent that they were more or less unbeatable in the competitions at which the AMOC had become unparalleled in organising – sprints, hillclimbs and short-duration track racing events.

Richard Stewart Williams saw it differently. He had been an apprentice at the Feltham works in his youth; later

he had, after an association (genuine) with Peter Sellers, started his own business in Brixton, tucked away under a railway arch in Padfield Road, from where I remember buying an engine for my unpowered DB4. He knew as much about the marque as anyone and had a great following among club members in the London area (and elsewhere) at the time when the works were, shall we say, less than diligent at supporting the owners of the DB4-6 models.

Williams's idea was to do to the DB4 what had been done to the DB4GT chassis in terms of making it lighter, but without shortening it. It did not stop there. Williams had helped to prepare John Goaté's racing 4GT and had made some fairly radical (for a road car) adjustments to it. The spirit of these was what he put into the 15 DB4s that he modified. They were much lighter than 4GTs, but used a bored-out

engine of up to 4.2 litres (which the works had done years before), and the suspension geometry was radically altered. They were in no sense road cars, with racing seats, roll-cages and huge extractor exhausts, but Williams proved that the DB4 could be made to go more or less as fast as you liked. As a DB4 owner, I was delighted. One day...

As the cars set new standards, so the protests began, but it was clear that just as contemporary road cars can learn from racing, so can old ones. These cars were not cheap by any measure, but they encapsulated such a vast resource of experience that people merely sat back and enjoyed them.

A lightweight DB4 Club Racer at Thruxton. The output of these Marek engines, tuned by specialists such as R. S. Williams, easily outstrips the original DB4 GT units.

The front aspect of the DB4. On this restored car the lack of overriders, large bonnet scoop and simple grille are clearly seen.

in synthetic oils and additives, which are as good at the time of writing as they have ever been, have in turn made an elderly Aston Martin as practical a proposition now as it has ever been, perhaps more so.

But David Brown had cars to sell, which is why the new alloy unit was fitted, be-Webered and in 3.9-litre form, almost straightaway into the DBR2 sports racer. And despite the Polish engineer's reservations, Aston Martin won with it first time out at Goodwood on 7 April 1958.

It is a very good engine, this, despite some obviously slapdash details, which, although they can be ironed out now, are nonetheless irritating and, to the uninitiated, disappointing. A good example is the inaccuracy with which the manifolds align to the

ports, which obviously impedes mixture flow. Another is the tendency for the head gasket to let oil ooze out at the front timing cover. With a few modifications, however, 300bhp is easily achievable after a rebuild, much of this by relatively straightforward re-engineering and blueprinting. One privateer has bored and stroked a DB4 engine to 5½ litres to produce 450bhp, which was brave of him.

The chassis of the DB4 is a massive affair, its huge strength allowing a particularly light body. The initial plan for the prototype had been for a DP114-type frame, but the body designers at Carrozzeria Touring of Milan disagreed. They knew – because it was their business to know – that alloy coachwork of the kind that they made, supported by a cage of steel tubes, needed proper support. They felt, rightly, that the DB2/4 chassis, a square tube-type, was not rigid enough. The result was that the DB4 chassis was hurried into production and, better safe than sorry, was rather heavier than it needed to be, but nonetheless comfortingly strong. In fact, the chassis was really very little changed, except in details, until the Virage, which illustrates eloquently the core soundness of Beach's work.

The floorpan is made from 18 gauge steel, pressed with a swage to add stiffness and with two 6-inch-deep box section sills MIG-welded to it. At the rear, the support for the rear seat, the tank and the rear suspension is a complex unit made internally from 16 gauge steel and skinned in 18. This area is the vulnerable one from the point of view of corrosion. At the front the cradle that supports both the engine and the running gear is massively strong, built up from ⅛-inch steel plate, and is linked to the front

bulkhead via 16 gauge box sections. The chassis were manufactured at the David Brown tractor plant at Farsley, in West Yorkshire. It shows.

The cage that supports the bodywork is of ⅝-inch-diameter 18 gauge steel tube and defines the main contours of the car's shape. This is the essence of the Superleggera technique. Although the cage is very strong, with certain spaceframe properties, the main strength of the car is drawn from the chassis.

The 16 gauge bodywork is of aluminium/magnesium alloy; it was pressed into approximate shape, then rolled and beaten on to formers before being attached. It is clenched around folded steel apertures that are welded to the steel cage, outlining the windscreens, bonnet, boot and doors. Under the alloy, where it meets the steel, is cloth tape, for the purposes of both sound

The basically clean design of the DB4 is most evident in profile.

The DB4 loses little of its elegance with the roof taken out, but a little rigidity.

and electrolytic insulation. Likewise the cage itself is wrapped. Moisture, of course, will simply speed up the electrolytic process, so if the tape becomes wet, be warned – it serves as an excellent conductor.

The Superleggera method is an Italian classic, but is time-consuming and expensive to execute. The Touring company of Milan, whose patent it was, went bankrupt in 1966, but the cars were not made there; the process was licensed by Aston Martin and the work done at Feltham, and later at Newport Pagnell.

Signor Bianchi, the chief stylist at Touring, initially produced a design that owed much in minor cosmetic details to previous work carried out on the DB2/4 'spyder', but which was simplified and cleaned up a little for production. The first scale model

shows a slightly 'Bedford van' treatment at the front and rather fussy rear lamps, but the overall proportions of the car were more or less unchanged; it was perhaps Bianchi's finest work to date, although his Lancia Flaminia coupé must run it a close second. In short, he got it right first time. In all this he was ably assisted by Federico Formenti.

So, Harold Beach, with his strong but hasty chassis design, did more than many to make the reputation of the Aston Martin in the eyes of the Goldfinger generation: compact, weighty and fast, but with an added margin of safety in hand over certain of the competition. Unimaginative? Perhaps. Over-engineered? Almost certainly. Owners are stunned when they discover how much weight can be safely pared off a DB4 chassis to prepare it for racing. It is the most

DB4 evolution

Series 1

October 1958–February 1960
149 cars built
Chassis numbers: DB4/101 to DB4/250
From chassis number:

131 – Window lift gearing raised; channel modified

151 – Sundym rear light offered; window frames fitted, curved glass; overriders and heavier bumpers fitted

161 – Hardura floor covering replaced with carpet

181 – First gear synchromesh cone added

191 – Gearbox mainshaft locking screw added

201 – Alloy fan cowl fitted; dashboard and engine wiring harness modified; bonnet scoop grille moved forward.

Series 2

February 1960–April 1961
349 cars built
Chassis numbers: DB4/251 to DB4/600
From chassis number:

251 – Sump enlarged to 17 pints; dipstick lengthened; engine mounts modified; dowels of flywheel housing lengthened; two dowels on timing cover replace single dowel; water pump fixing stud lengthened; top front oilway on block enlarged; big-end nuts no longer castellated; oil pressure relief valve spring strengthened; cam covers replaced; camshaft bearing clearances revised; timing case changed; oil pump output increased; vacuum advance fitted; dynamo bracket revised; upper wishbone location to kingpin modified; front brake discs enlarged from 11½ inches to 12⅛ inches; front brake callipers now Dunlop VB1075

(VB1033); front pads now VB05084 (VB05089); check valve to servo pipe modified; servo mounting clamp modified; vacuum hose from manifold reinforced; check valve ¼-inch nut now Nylok (Avlock); disc shields enlarged; front and rear calliper bridge pipes modified; circlips deleted from pedal pivot shaft; master cylinder bracket bolts rearranged; pedal pushrods modified; radiator blind fitted; bulkhead grommets modified; heater front case assembly modified; bonnet rehung with front hinges; flat window glass introduced; flat rear quarterlight introduced; alloy retainer for quarterlight seal improved; door lock remote rods strengthened; door glass cant rails deleted; door waist rail weatherstrip improved; door pillar seal strip replaced by extrusion; gearing on window winder raised; oil cooler introduced as option; overdrive becomes option; electric window lifts become option; wiper arms modified; rear ashtrays fitted

267 – Crankcase breather fitted on nearside engine mount

390 – Crank pulley modified; dynamo pulley modified

550 – Oil strainer modified

570 – Sump capacity raised to 21 pints.

Series 3

April 1961–September 1961
164 cars built
Chassis numbers: DB4/601 to DB4/765
From chassis number:

601 – Cam cover breathers modified; electric rev counter fitted; five demister vents replace three; indicator/flasher switch now single; choke cable clamps modified; twin bonnet props introduced; handbrake pads now detachable from

backplates; oil strainer modified again; distributor advance curve modified; coil changed; solenoid changed; horn and headlamp relay modified; close-ratio gearbox introduced; 4.09:1 axle offered; courtesy lights fitted; brake callipers upgraded; gearbox layshaft rollers modified; rear lamp cluster changed to three lenses; protective shield fitted around pedal box; GT engine option listed

696 – First gear bearing bush revised

701 – Crankcase breather moved to timing cover

759 – Second gear synchromesh cone modified.

Series 4

September 1961–October 1962
314 cars built
Chassis numbers: DB4/766 to DB4/950*
From chassis number:

766 – Air scoop lowered and grille deleted; radiator grille changed to bar type; starter ring and flywheel modified; GT twin-plate clutch introduced; flywheel housing modified; coil changed; ballast resistor fitted; ashtray moved from dash to gearbox cover; rear light cluster revised; rear bumper bar fitted with reflectors; Lucas numberplate lamp replaced by Hella; 3.3:1 axle standardised for non-overdrive cars; oil cooler now standard; separate intake fitted for oil cooler; Special Series engine introduced

839 – Special Series engine first fitted

943 – Close-ratio gearbox now optional; Armstrong Selectaride dampers offered

951 – Cowled headlamps offered as option; DB4 Vantage introduced; ammeter moved to top centre of instrument binnacle; dynamo modified; DB4GT instrument panel offered.

Series 5

September 1962–June 1963
134 cars built
Chassis numbers: DB4/1001 to DB4/1050*
From chassis number:

1001 – Body lengthened to 15 feet (4.57 metres); roofline raised; 15-inch wheels fitted; Special Series engine now standard; cold air box fitted to carburettors; electric fan fitted in front of radiator; automatic transmission offered; brake callipers modified; advance curve modified; ignition switch modified; GT instrument panel now standard; ammeter and fuse boxes modified; most cars now have cowled lamps

1066 – Overdrive gearbox now wide ratio as standard

1175 – Rev counter drive unit modified

1176 – Twin filler flaps offered

* Convertibles (not, please, Volantes) used three groups of chassis numbers: the Series 4 cars used DB4C/1051 to DB4C/1080 and the Series 5 cars DB4C/1081 to DB4C/1110 and DB4C/1166 to DB4C/1175.

Further, there was a secondary type, the Vantage. Series 4 Vantage saloons, using the Special Series engine, used chassis numbers DB4/951 to DB4/995. Series 5 Vantage saloons used chassis numbers DB4/1111 to DB4/1165 and DB4/1176 to DB4/1215. Most (but not all) of these cars had faired–in headlamps.

A total of 32 convertibles were fitted with Special Series engines and at least one received a GT twin-plug engine.

popular basis for a racer, too, being the lightest of the Newport Pagnell cars.

The steering and suspension were also new departures. Rack-and-pinion replaced the steering box of the DB2 series, and a supple wishbone front suspension, damped by Armstrong shock absorbers, replaced the worthy, but by comparison crude, torsion bar equipment of the previous model. At the rear, coil springs and lever arm dampers appeared, while a live axle located by parallel arms and a Watt linkage were also introduced. The location of the axle is good enough, actually, although there are always those who say it is crude; it has reliability on its side, whereas the later, more complex de Dion layout has its drawbacks with hard use.

Also extraordinary is the amount of the chassis that can simply oxidise and fall off without hinting to the proud owner that all is not well with the car. In this way many DB4s, 5s and 6s have survived in apparently pristine condition, and although most of them were attended to in the 1980s, when enthusiasm for the marque scaled new heights, there are always those cars that have lurked on the margins, and which are, to all intents and purposes, untouched. Originality often has its price, and these cars were not designed to last for ever. The fact that so many are still around is a tribute to their constructors.

In terms of driveability, the DB4 scores heavily over its predecessors in several key areas. The immense rigidity of the chassis and the accurate rear axle location offered by the parallel trailing arms and Watt linkage allow the power of the Marek engine to be applied with some confidence. The steering, while not pin-sharp (the car is too heavy for that), is precise and well-geared. The front suspension, another Beach design, is first-rate.

The trademark air vent, continued to this day. It is, for some reason, the most instantly recognisable feature of the DB4/5/6.

The indirect gear performance of the DB4 must have been a revelation in 1958. The square, torquey engine, with a very light flywheel – an Aston trademark – revs quickly. Its power, transmitted through a robust (some say 'agricultural') David Brown gearbox to a live rear axle can be put down quite effectively, although the car will tend to become tail-happy if abused. In fact, I have found that a David Brown 'box will accept most of the abuse that can be thrown at it, so it is unlikely to let you down. The light coachwork and massive chassis offer a low centre of gravity, so the car remains manoeuvrable at high speed until the aerodynamics reach their limit.

The final iteration of the rear lamps.

The DB4 is a good but agile cruiser. With a standard final drive of 3.54:1 it will amble along at 90–100mph with no great drama. On secondary roads, using second and third gears, the car comes alive with the engine on cam, and while it is no lightweight, it handles like a much smaller car. Indeed, like all Astons, the whole thing shrinks around you quite rapidly once you become accustomed to it. There is one difficulty, and one that a driver obeying speed limits is unlikely to discover, which is that the car, for all its beauty, is a little light at the back at high speed. Despite a theoretical maximum of 148mph (with the right axle), the car feels skittish at over 120.

Do not expect too much from the axle: the Salisbury 4HA, with or

without a Powr-Lok limited-slip diff, is a sound device, but has frequently been neglected. It is prone to wear, and although the lash can be adjusted out relatively easily, many previous owners will not have bothered. Character, you see...

Finding the room to exploit the engine's strengths is the problem, as it was to be for all road Aston Martins after this one. Although in standard form the engine is not peaky, above 4,000rpm is where the power really comes in and, with only four gears, one is not exactly spoiled for choice. Clearly the DB4 is a car built for unrestricted roads. In fact, I have found that fourth gear is almost irrelevant, as the car is almost idling at motorway speeds. As for the overdrive (which was optional on cars with 3.77:1 or 4.09:1 axles), it is more or less unnecessary now. Except in Germany.

On crossply tyres the car can tramline. Recommended tyre pressures are probably on the low side, so a little more air can alleviate the trait. The use of radial tyres is a matter of choice, but I found that they offered a great improvement. My first DB4, a Series 4, wore Goodyears, which were only available in 15-inch size and meant the use of later wheels from the Series 5. (This had obvious benefits in acceleration, with a smaller rolling radius, but I never did get round to recalibrating the speedometer.) Pirelli radials are available in 16-inch application, but their cost is high. I think that things have improved a little from those days, and folk speak highly of Yokahama 16-inch radials. However, purists will probably insist on the traditional Avons or Dunlops. Some of them will also want to use the original air in them.

It would also be a mistake to expect too much of the brakes, however startling they were when new. They are, after all, old technology, and a further caution is that the leather

seats offer little in the way of lateral support so that the driver can seem to be holding on to the steering wheel as if it were a grab handle. With conventional seat belts it is hard to strap oneself in tightly; the result can be very poor location for the driver on tight roads. The only real answer is bucket seats and a proper harness. The lack of headrests (and often seat belts) is a time-warp.

All in all, the DB4, like most Astons, is at its best on long sweeping bends where its sheer grunt can be released to the full. It is a good cross-country car; indeed, there are few better of this layout, but in heavy traffic it can be something of an ordeal. The well-weighted steering hardens up at low speeds and the huge clutch pedal pressure becomes tiresome. To be stuck in traffic is difficult if there is no electric fan, and rear visibility from the steeply raked rear screen, particularly in the wet, is less than

The DB4 is a good touring car, but hell in traffic

perfect. The wipers are, well, dreadful. Also, the windows steam up, or perhaps that is the driver.

We are, of course, spoiled by modern hatchbacks when it comes to the urban driving experience. The DB4 is one of those vehicles whose few faults become glaring when inching through a big city. It can become very hot inside and the exhaust noise, such a pleasure on the open road, becomes intrusive. In a high state of tune the engine can seem lumpy at low revs and the plugs have a slight

Right:
The gaping maw of an early DB4. The earliest cars had their crank breathers low on the block.

The Special Series DB4 engine. Not all cars fitted with this are known as DB4 Vantages, as it was an optional extra from 1961.

tendency to oil up. Twin-cam engines often burn more oil than seems reasonable (the Jaguar XK is another good example) and the Aston 'six', operating on such vast internal pressures, can also be profligate, particularly if it is a tired example.

A union dispute delayed the start of production until a year after the car's announcement, but the lag was not, it seems, sufficient to iron out some of the problems concerning prolonged high-speed running. Basically, there was not enough oil in the engine, and what was there was not moving quickly enough. Extended tests up and down the newly opened M1 motorway failed to reveal the problem, partly because the ambient temperature was not high enough to be critically important.

When production finally got under

way, some of the earliest casualties of the weakness were found in France. At that time France was Aston Martin's third biggest client base, not to mention the number of Brits barrelling down the Routes Nationales to the south, and the pleas for help started to come thick and fast. It was a poor start to what at that time was the most civilised GT car that the world had seen.

Development of the DB4 was rather ad hoc. The first 50 cars (chassis numbers start at DB4/101) had rear-hinged bonnets, no window frames and very slim bumper bars. Overheating difficulties (of which more later) led to the introduction of an alloy cowl for the engine fan at chassis 201. At the same time the bonnet scoop was moved forward.

The DB4 evolved, retrospectively, into

five semi-distinct series. They were only ever DB4s at the factory, and the Aston Martin Owners' Club has divided them up as shown in the accompanying table. The categories are not, however, cast in stone, and many intermediary types are found, which confuses the issue. The AMOC template is a useful one, however, so we shall stick with it. Having found a DB4, one needs to work out where it fits into the life of the model.

These production variations, apart from gradually increasing the oil capacity and modifying engine bearing clearances and cooling, were mainly minor and cosmetic, until the Series 5 car, which became in effect the same size as the DB5 as the body length was increased. The DB4 Series 5 Vantage is almost indistinguishable from the DB5 itself, the last ones even having the DB5's twin fuel filler flaps.

However, there are always inconsistencies to be found, such as Series 3 cars with Special Series

A 'show engine'. The lacquered dashpots, polished camboxes and gloss finish suggest that this is a Motor Show-prepared DB4 Special Series.

The DB4 was trimmed to an unheard-of level of sophistication (for 1958).

engines or a Vantage saloon with an unmodified front end. Many cars will also have undergone modification by owners, enthusiasts, engineers, or the factory. Record-keeping was always terrible at Feltham and Newport Pagnell, but the build sheets do exist, and can be accessed via the good offices of Aston Service Dorset, who

acquired manufacturing rights for pre-DB4 models from Company Developments in 1972.

It is a sign of originality that the engine number approximates to the chassis number, so a late car with a low engine number is almost certain to have had a replacement engine. There is nothing wrong with this, of course, as not everyone enjoys the economic privilege that permits a new engine. Engine numbers are prefixed by capacity and suffixed by number, as in 370/958. A Special Series engine is suffixed SS.

The chassis number can be found all over the place. A riveted plate on the right front of the engine compartment is the most obvious place to look, but the factory identification will be found on the left-hand lower chassis near the bottom wishbone or the top door hinge on the left-hand side, and the bonnet hinges will also be stamped. Further, the reverse side of

The dash is similar to that of the Mark III, the instrument binnacle echoing the type introduced with that model. Ergonomically, it works well.

the door panels and rear seat backs will have the number chalked on them if the upholstery is original, and quite possibly if it is not. Bear in mind that many swaps will have taken place over the years; better to have nice soft seats from another car, rather than wait ten years for the re-trim to mellow. Finally, avoid nasty plastic re-trims.

The nicest DB4 to look at, convertibles aside, is probably the first one. The best all-round car, however, is probably the Series 4 Vantage with the Special Series

engine, before the car put on weight to become the Series 5. It has all the merits of the early car, but its engine is by now almost bomb-proof. The absolute ideal is a DB4 with a GT engine, but these 'Vantage GTs' are very rare indeed – the rarest of all DB4s.

The DB4 made a huge impression when it arrived on the scene in October 1958. It was built in parallel with the Mk III until July 1959, when the last example of the DB2 line was produced and concentration turned to the first all-new model created under the auspices of the David Brown Group.

It owed nothing to the DB2 series, being built with a new chassis, a new body and a new engine. The first mainstream road test of the DB4, published in the American journal *Road and Track*, appeared in May 1959, artfully (and well) written by Roy Salvadori, the Aston Martin works driver, who would win at Le Mans the next month.

All in all, the DB4 is a great car. If looked after, indeed subtly modified,

The dashboard of the drophead; this is a well-known concours-winning car.

particularly if made to run on lead-free fuel, it is a real joy to own, notwithstanding its few age-related drawbacks. It is elegant, fast and involving, in the way that for example a Porsche is, a Maserati or a Ferrari is, and a Jensen will never be.

The DB4 convertible, announced at the London Motor Show in 1961, is probably the prettiest of the line, but in practical terms is slightly handicapped by the lack of rigidity imposed upon the rest of the structure by the removal of the roof. It is, however, a rare example of how the same car can look just as elegant with or without a roof. A hardtop was available, which gave it a very Maserati 3500 coupé look from the rear. This is unsurprising: the Touring company designed both. The Lancia Flaminia drophead, although slightly flashier, shares the same basic proportions, as does the Alfa 2600 Spider, that under-engined but vastly underrated car. But none of them has quite the same combination of delicacy coupled with uncompromising grunt that really defines the Anglo-Italian phase of Aston Martin's history. The design of the drophead was entirely Touring's work; they increased the torsional rigidity of the chassis by over a third, but this does not prevent surface cracking of the body between the rear filler flaps and the hood aperture, a function of the tiny distance between the two. Otherwise, the DB4 convertible is pleasingly rigid.

The visual trick that all these cars play arises from their total lack of adornment: there is no superfluous trim, everything is there for a purpose, and the visual proportions are uninterrupted by stylistic frippery. As a result they appear to be lighter than they really are, and do not attract particular attention. Compare a DB4 with its contemporary Facel Vega, for example, and the full effect is seen. Get inside, and feel the total inertia of the thing until the engine is started. Then it begins to come to life.

A DB4 is still one of the prettiest things on the road.

Buying Hints

Be careful. The DB4 is a uniquely good car, but there is a series of traps for the unwary. These points also apply to the DB5 and DB6.

1. The sheer robustness of the chassis allows for a huge attrition of the metal before the whole structure becomes unreliable. Particular points at which this happens are, from the front, the pedal box, the jacking points, the sills, the door bottoms, the anchorage tubes for the sturdy trailing arms, and the upper assembly that locates the Watt linkage behind the seat. The spare wheel well can also tear itself out, with embarrassing consequences, and the rear passenger floor, where moisture can puddle in the pressed swages, is also vulnerable, but less critical.

At the very front, accident damage aside, the story is cheerier. The massive cradle that carries the engine could be a spare part from a cruiser, so few concerns there. This is easily inspected and its alignment checked.

It all sounds horrendous, but the only really inaccessible part is the sill structure, and even then a thin screwdriver can do wonders, even if it only makes the guilty vendor blanch upon its production. Be in no doubt that a sound chassis should be prized above all things. Paintwork, to an extent, will be a function of the chassis.

2. Alloy will not 'rust', of course, but the electrolytic action between alloy and steel is no small thing; the alloy is corrupted by it and turns cheesy and horrid. There is no solution apart from patch-welding, which is both expensive and unpredictable. It further suggests

A full DB4 rebuild is not for the faint-hearted.

that the steel underneath also requires attention; until that is rectified, bodywork repairs are just something on the shopping list.

3. Be prepared to put up with a visual check for filler, as obviously a magnet will not work. These cars had no filler on them when new, merely a smear of cellulose stopper. If there is filler, the car has been repaired, and it has probably been done on the cheap. Due to the flexing of the body, which is designed in, filler will not stay where it is put for ever, which is why there was none of it in the first place. Compare the Aston Martin with its contemporary Ferrari, for example, and you will see that the beaten-out alloy of the Ferrari is loaded with body filler, and almost certainly was when new.

4. The interior will speak for itself. Small tears and abrasions are neither

here nor there, but it can be useful to check the obverse of a trim panel to see if the chassis number is present, probably scribbled in chalk or wax crayon. It should match the vehicle ID. Given that the interiors are hand-made, repair and replacement is straightforward, if costly.

5. Running gear checks, apart from ensuring that the trailing arms are attached as they should be and that the brakes work, are few. The sockets in the chassis that accept the rear arm of the lower front wishbone are split aluminium inserts. They can corrode, destroy themselves and become jammed; they are only protected from the elements by a wired-on plastic cover, and repair is costly. Likewise, there should be securing straps that hold the steering rack down, which only matter if the rack comes adrift; they look rather home-made, and are really, being something of an afterthought.

6. The engine of a DB4 is its most beguiling feature. It is beautifully presented, and a glance will tell you what it is. It will have either two or three SU carburettors. It should have single chromed nuts holding the cam boxes to the head. If the nuts are paired, and there are triple carburettors, then it is a head (or an engine) from a later car, a 5, 6 or DBS. It is not rare to find later heads grafted on to DB4 engines and, indeed, some people do it for choice; it has the effect of dropping the compression ratio a little and improving torque. If the engine is fitted with Webers, they are replacements.

7. The engine should have vast oil pressure. If it has been rebuilt, the gauge should indicate something around 100psi at 3,000rpm. If the pressure is volatile, ask why, or mentally deduct from the asking price the cost of finding out. It is important also to test the engine under load, if only to discover whether both halves of the feeble SU fuel pump work. If they do not, a mechanical emphysema at over 4,000rpm will tell you. If the car has no oil cooler, make a mental note to fit one. If it has one, make a mental note to fit a bigger one. Many early DB4s ran their bearings and lunched their blocks, and the observant will have noticed that they are no longer under warranty.

8. The propensity for the engines to generate, and become clogged by, sludge around the iron cylinder liners

is not uniformly distributed down the length of the block. The rear half of the engine is more prone to do this, exacerbating a slack spot in water circulation (the water pump is at the front). Ideally, a rebuilt engine should have had its liners pulled out to allow a comprehensive clean-up of the waterways, but the recommended method of doing this requires total immersion in a hot tank in order that the alloy, which expands faster than the cast iron, can release its grip evenly. You can imagine that this is something of an ordeal for the home restorer. I have seen blocks heated with an air blower to accomplish the same thing, but purists will say that the procedure is dubious, with an obvious risk of distortion and the consequent need for re-machining. One thing is sure. Pulling the liners out cold will require equipment of Goliath-like proportions and probably damage the block, so is not a realistic option.

9. Driving the car in order to evaluate it is usually left to an expert, but there are some basic checks that anyone can make. First, valve noise, which should comprise a gentle gnashing, with no discernible clatters. Quick throttle response is a feature of these engines, so expect it. If the vendor says that 'it needs a bit of a tune', give him an old-fashioned look. Water temperature and oil pressure are vital, and do check if there is an electric fan fitted.

The crown wheel and pinion can be noisy on all Astons. They work hard and frankly seldom receive any attention. Sloppiness can be adjusted out and even rebuilds are not that costly, as all the parts are readily available. The 'Salisbury whine' can be heard on many cars,

and Astons are no different. Changing axle ratios is likewise not a problem.

10. Gearboxes are largely a matter of preference. Obviously they should not, for example, leap out of gear, nor should they make a huge noise, and the change should, when the oil is warm, be reasonably baulk-free and swift. Some clutch drag is not a catastrophe and the engine note may vary marginally if the clutch is in or out, but no serious points should be deducted.

11. A quick run backwards can be revealing. If the tail end lifts alarmingly, the trailing arm bushes are at least sloppy, or shot, or the axle is physically adrift at the Watt linkage. Any doubts should be confirmed by a visual check. Accept no excuses: if this sort of thing does take place, the car to which it happens is an MoT failure waiting to cost you an awful lot of money.

If, after all the foregoing, you think that the car is a reasonable prospect, short-list it for a going-over by an expert. What you have missed, they should tell you.

As to whether these cars are suitable for home restoration, it rather depends on how competent you are. The recommissioning of components such as carburettors or electrical equipment is hardly a major undertaking, and brake parts, starter motor, dynamo and fuel pump (don't repair it – change it) are well within the skills of the average home restorer. As to serious welding and engine rebuilds, it is probably better to be your own clerk of works and find the specialists, unless you want a restoration which is 'all of a piece' – tremendous if you can afford it.

The Lagonda *Rapide*

David Brown always liked the Lagonda marque, but in the face of opposition from a host of sturdily well-built saloon cars from other manufacturers, it was always a slow seller. The 2½-3 litre class was a hotly contested marketplace and the introduction of the Jaguar Mark I effectively killed off the dull but worthy Lagonda 3 litre. Lagondas were, particularly in comparison to the Coventry product, always very expensive for what they were. They were not, of course, selling into a market exactly obsessed by value for money, so that criticism is merely made in passing. It is not how I judge cars; if it was, I would drive a Trabant.

The decision to reintroduce the famous Rapide name was Brown's and Brown's alone. John Wyer, the General Manager at Aston Martin from 1956, was very dubious, as was Harold Beach, but the latter was at least pleased that the proposed new car would have a de Dion rear axle, a fitment for which he had already lobbied when working on the DB4. The reduction in unsprung weight afforded by such a layout would go some way to compensate for the overall bulk of the new car. For it was big. The wheelbase was 16 inches (406mm) longer than that of the DB4, the track 3½ inches (89mm) wider and the overall dry weight was up by 750lb (341kg).

The poor old Lagonda Rapide, a worthy if much maligned and underdeveloped car. Commercially it was a lemon, although it has its fans now.

The bodywork was, like that of its sibling, of the Superleggera type, and styled by Touring of Milan. The original drawings show early DB4 rear lamps, shared with the contemporary Alvis, and a distinctly DB4-like front. Had that design been adhered to, and the underpinnings been sorted, there can be little doubt that the Lagonda Rapide would have gone down in history as a desirable classic, in the mould of the Bentley Flying Spur. The fact that the Rapide is considerably rarer rather says it all.

Sadly, an ad hoc styling committee at Aston Martin had a hand in affairs. What they came up with left the rear of the car alone, with the exception of updating the rear lamps, but at the front the Touring design was replaced with a truly dreadful snout, flanked by twin headlights and reminiscent of Ford's ghastly Edsel; there was no discernible Lagonda theme in the radiator grille treatment. Well, everyone is entitled to at least one mistake. This was Brown's.

So, frowning and aggressive, the Rapide made its entrance at the 1961 Motor Show and David Brown sat back and waited for the order book to fill up. Happily, he did not hold his breath. Certainly some of his friends ordered them, but over the entire production life of the car, only 55 were sold.

But the car had certain things going for it: it was undeniably exclusive, beautifully put together and technically advanced. In protracted use, however, spline wear was heavy as a result of the angle of exit of the driveshafts to the rear wheels, and while the car was quick and agile for one of its size and specification, the engine, bored out to 4 litres in preparation for an upgrade to the DB4, was under-carburetted. The use of twin Solex PH44 twin-choke carburettors was an odd one, as they were both costly and inefficient. The use of a maximum of four chokes on a six-cylinder engine gave mixture tuning problems at speed, and while

The main reason for its unpopularity are the visuals, which are, to say the least, an acquired taste.

an SU set-up was offered for those owners who opted for the DB4 Special Series engine (basically, one could order what one wanted), the Rapides equipped with the Solex equipment were relatively sluggish by comparison.

Further, a car of this type begged for automatic transmission; the choice of the Borg-Warner Model 8 variety was also probably a mistake as it was totally unsuited to the slightly strangled power curve of the engine, just as it would be in all other Aston Martin applications up to and including the DBS. It is even possible that too many were ordered in anticipation of the Rapide's sales; the David Brown range was certainly blighted by them for some time. In this application, it really is a useless piece of kit.

A Rapide interior: very much the grand style.

had some ambitions in the North American market where such styling was and is less controversial.

As things turned out, however, the Lagonda Rapide was commercially a lemon, and that is a pity. It was a classic British might-have-been. For its price it should have been nigh perfect. It should have been (and don't laugh) an upmarket British version of that most competent of cars, the Borgward Isabella – the car that could do most things, and finally broke the company – but the Rapide was merely a distraction for Aston Martin.

You feel a twit without a chauffeur – it's lonely in there

Interestingly enough, later on in the story there was some thought of reinventing the concept of the Rapide, the powerful four-wheeled drawing-room, by fitting an Alvis TF21 with an Aston Martin engine. There is still one around somewhere and it is probably a much better car so equipped. But those cart springs...

Aston Martin persisted with the Rapide until 1964. It was a disappointment to Brown, but he was philosophical. He knew that his firm was not competing with Daimler-Benz, or Rolls-Royce (or even Alvis, really), and the marque, being now an Aston derivative, could hardly be expected to command any 'brand loyalty'. If people wanted one of David Brown's cars, they simply bought an Aston Martin. If they weren't particular, they bought two Jaguars.

So, while a Special Series-engined Rapide with the David Brown manual box is a seriously viable option (once you have worked out who is going to buy it from you when you tire of it), a Solexed automatic is a fairly dodgy prospect. Converting such a car to a better specification is always going to be a marginal exercise, although one or two have been brought up to manual DB6 Vantage levels, so if you try one, be selective. Our cheery psychopath will, if selling to you, probably divert your attention to the car's rarity, its build quality, comfort and the luvverly levver seats. If buying from you, he probably won't want to close the deal, citing the complete unsaleability of the cars.

The one I owned, a manual 4-litre with Solex carburettors, went very well, it seemed to me, with the rear end well tied down and an overall good level of ride. There was no discernible rumble from the dreaded spline syndrome, about which everyone will tell you, but for obvious reasons one is unavoidably drawn to comparison with a Jaguar Mk II. However, I must say that, having

driven both, I rather preferred the Lagonda, not that I ever thrashed it. Never mind that a rear axle overhaul is mind-numbingly expensive, or that a broken windscreen would also break the bank, it was lovely. The interior alone was worth buying the car for, complete with picnic tables and lashings of walnut. The front seats are thoroughly Mercedes-like and very supportive, although the bench rear might as well have been designed to cause maximum dislocation on bends. You just feel a bit of a twit without a chauffeur; it's lonely in there.

Whether it compares as well to the Jaguar S-Type, which is in most ways superior to the Mark II and will take everything a ham-fisted driver can dish out, is another matter, but that would not be a fair comparison anyway, as the S-Type is a later design. No, I liked the Lagonda; it was one of the first fast four-door saloons that I had ever driven and, looks aside, it knocked spots off an Alvis TD21 with its cart springs and an engine built by the same firm that made the Town Hall clock. If only Aston Martin had left the front treatment alone and left it to the Italians (or anybody, for that matter) all would have been well, but Brown

Formula 1

If it seems strange that Aston Martin had not made a serious assault on the world of grand prix racing by the late 1950s, the answer is money. That is, lack of it. Brown wanted to do it, of course, but the crippling expense of sports car racing, coupled with the fact that the road cars were barely breaking even as a business, prevented him from making a serious foray into that most addictive of sports.

Not that he didn't try. The advent of the 2½-litre formula for the 1954 season led Aston to develop a single-seater car based on the DB3S chassis. This car, DP155, was never to race in the top echelons, but did enter several Formule Libre events in New Zealand in the hands of Reg Parnell.

A more serious car, a subset of the DBR1, was started in 1955 and ready for testing in late 1957. It was also good, and while it lacked the wind-cheating qualities of the Vanwall, it was competitive with the then current Ferrari Dino and Maserati 250F. Roy Salvadori, who drove for Cooper in Formula 1 in 1957 (indeed, scored the first championship points for the little rear-engined Cooper Climax that year), was fairly certain that the car would have an edge for the 1958 season. And Salvadori knew his stuff.

But priorities intervened. David Brown could not afford to participate in both grand prix and sports car races, so the Formula 1 project, DBR4, sat around until the opportunity came to enter it and support it properly. But times were changing – Moss won the Argentine Grand Prix in a privately entered Cooper in January 1958 and, despite the fact that the front-engined Vanwall won the Constructors' Championship that year, the last of

the type to do so, the writing was on the wall for front-engined cars.

Brown reconsidered in April 1959. Two DBR4s were completed for grand prix events that year, to be driven by Salvadori and Shelby. Salvadori came second in the International Trophy race at Silverstone, which was encouraging, and two fine sixth places in the British and Portuguese Grands Prix tended to confirm his initial opinion. Three were built.

The DBR5 that followed was in many ways a great leap sideways with an undeveloped independent rear suspension, although the veteran Maurice Trintignant, Shelby's replacement, achieved two finishes with the car in 1960.

Aston's foray into Formula 1 was not a success. This is a DBR4, photographed in the early 1980s.

So, who knows? Had the Formula 1 cars been raced and developed earlier, perhaps things would have been different. Perhaps AML would have gone bankrupt, too, although sponsorship was just around the corner. But the Formula 1 episode was not the end of Aston Martin's racing ambitions.

Aston Martin DB4GT

It was not long before the temptation to raise their game a little proved irresistible to Aston Martin. Because the preliminary tests on the twin-plug version of Marek's engine had been extremely promising, they knew that the unit could be developed further, at least in terms of output; reliability was slightly more of an unknown quantity. They further knew that in road form the DB4 was longer than it needed to be as a sports car and, consequently, heavier.

This was due partly to Beach's natural caution and partly to engineering overkill brought on by lack of time. Work commenced to increase power and, more straightforwardly, reduce weight. This second imperative was easy; the core material was hardly short of avoirdupois. It was a classic opportunity to put into effect that marvellous American expression, 'simplicate and add lightness'.

To lower the overall weight of the car, the chassis was shortened by 5 inches (127mm) and the gauge of

Stirling Moss in DP199, the prototype DB4GT, at Silverstone in 1959.

the body was reduced in parts; this saved roughly 190lb (86kg). The front suspension and steering were left untouched and the rear suspension softened somewhat. Axle ratios were as for the DB4. Naturally, Beach's chassis, when shortened, was even more rigid than before, which was a

The DB4GT astonished those who drove it

major advantage for the DB4GT, given the pounding that the type would receive. In fact, it could have been a lot lighter, but in the 1950s safety was perceived to be largely a matter of strength. In an accident there was no consideration of clever crumple zones or built-in deformable sections; the objective was more to maintain the shape of the thing as it tumbled across the landscape. In the event of colliding with another vehicle, that vehicle became the enemy, as it were.

The DB4GT made its debut at the London Motor Show in 1959. Its progenitor, DP199, had, in the hands of Stirling Moss, won on its first outing on 2 May at Silverstone, in the warm-up race for the *Daily Express* trophy. Fitted with a mandatory 3-litre version of the engine, the car retired at Le Mans the next month. Nonetheless, with the DB4 just starting to enter the public's consciousness, the new car's appearance was timely, if distracting.

The GT engine was fitted with both a twin-plug head and triple Weber carburettors. The bottom end of the engine, with the exception of polished rods and slightly higher-compression pistons, was unchanged. The brakes were upgraded to Girling units of a similar type to those employed by the racers, but with softer pads for road use.

Aston Martin DB4GT
September 1959–June 1963

ENGINE:
In-line six-cylinder, alloy block and head

Bore x stroke	92 x 92mm
Capacity	3670cc
Valves	Twin ohc
Compression ratio	9:1
Carburettors	Three Weber 45mm DCOs
Power	c300bhp at 6,000rpm

TRANSMISSION:
David Brown four-speed manual gearbox with Powr-Lok limited-slip differential standard. Ratio 3.54:1

SUSPENSION:
Coil springs all round as DB4, but rear spring deflection lower.
Front: Transverse wishbones, ball-jointed kingpins, anti-roll bar, Armstrong telescopic dampers
Back: Live axle, trailing arms, Watt linkage, Armstrong lever-arm dampers
Steering: Rack and pinion

BRAKES: Girling discs all round

WHEELS:
16-inch Dunlop centre-lock wires; 16-inch Borrani optional extra. Tyres 6.00 x 16-inch crossply

BODYWORK:
Bodywork and chassis as late DB4 but 5½ inches shorter. Some models had lighter gauge alloy. Cowled lamps.
19 cars were bodied by Zagato, one by Bertone

LENGTH:	14ft 3½in (4.36m)
WIDTH:	5ft 6in (1.68m)
WHEELBASE:	7ft 9in (2.36m)
HEIGHT:	4ft 3½in (1.31m)
WEIGHT:	25cwt (1,271kg)
MAX SPEED:	c150mph (241kph)
PRICE NEW:	£4,500
PRODUCTION FIGURES:	100

And that was that, really. A very straightforward set of modifications, only economically possible due to the essentially hand-built nature of the car, produced a machine of startling competence. Naturally, it was no more sophisticated than its progenitor, but the vital inches shaved off the chassis, coupled with a prodigious increase in power, produced a package that astonished those who drove it. It was and is amazingly quick.

Beach and company were not allowed to go the whole hog, however. Given his head, Beach would have opted for a de Dion rear end (just as he would have liked on the DB4), but the cost of manufacturing it to acceptable

The DB4GT Zagato: all cars should look like this

It was a glimpse of a Zagato-bodied Bristol 406 that triggered the idea of a limited run of special-bodied DB4GTs. The Milan firm, founded in 1919, had carved out for itself an enviable reputation for startling design (not always easy on the eye, as a glance at the Lancia Flavia Zagato will attest) that went back to the glorious Alfa Romeo 1750 and before. The plan was to ship completed chassis out to Milan, where they would be bodied in the Italian manner, beaten out rather than rolled, before being returned to Britain for trimming and finishing. Five cars were, in fact, fully completed and trimmed in Italy.

It was hoped that there might be some competition future for the new car; that it might be raced or sprinted by its (presumably affluent) owner. The was no need to homologate the type for racing since the DB4GT, as a DB4 variant, already was. In fact, the

The rear three-quarter view.

Zagato was a respectably successful racer, but of course was to come up against both the E-Type Jaguar and the hottest Ferraris of the 250 series, which, when all was said and done, gave away three-quarters of a litre to the Astons and still beat them.

The Zagatos were all different; each car was a subtle variant on a core

design drawn up by Ercole Spada, the young Zagato house designer. It was, in fact, one of his first projects, as he had not done the design on the Bristol chassis. Hugely influential, it was a seminal piece of work – 'fierce beyond belief' as John Bolster put it – and the basic proportions have survived the test of time. A second glance at a DB7 is often required if viewed from a certain angle, just to make sure.

The frontal aspect of the Zagato. 'Fierce beyond belief' as John Bolster put it.

The Zagato has a slightly more functional interior.

The Zagato was introduced at the 1960 London Motor Show at Earls Court to, unusually, universal acclaim. All agreed that the shape was jaw-droppingly lovely and the fact that it was only £900 more expensive than the DB4GT and £1,400 more than a DB4 would seem today to be irresistible; however, the gap has rather widened now, to the extent that a DB4GT is probably worth 2½ DB4s, and a Zagato weighs in at around six DB4GTs. The reason that the Zagato was a slow seller, with only 19 cars produced, was simple – the E-Type Jaguar. An Aston owner could have a DB4 and an E-Type for the price of the Zagato, and many, of course, did just that.

Despite its commercial failure, the Zagato has rightly achieved cult status. In mid-1991 the concept was re-introduced when four 'Sanction 2' cars were unveiled, as a result of the

co-operation between Aston Martin and Zagato on the V8 project. They used unallocated chassis numbers from the 1960s. Unallocated? Possibly. Unsold is more likely. Witnesses describe the eye-watering sight of unsold Zagato-bodied chassis undergoing the indignity of

being cut up with torches at Newport Pagnell and sold for scrap during the rush for cash during the recession of 1973.

The Zagato was certainly up against some tough opposition. On a performance basis it had the legs of a Maserati, but not a Ferrari, despite its superior chassis. Its British nemesis was, though, the E-Type Jaguar. It out-handled the E-Type, and was, with the right gearing, as quick in a straight line, but it was price that dictated the buyer's priority if exclusivity was not paramount. The purchase of two Jags, one a drophead and one a coupé, offered considerably more flexibility to someone with Aston Martin DB4GT money burning a hole in their pocket. The E-Type, despite its obvious shortcomings, became the benchmark by which all Grand Touring cars would be judged from here on.

The twin-plug Zagato engine is even more highly tuned.

road standards was too high. Even so, there can be little doubt that the DB4GT was, as a road car at least, probably the best of its type available. Certainly, the Ferrari 250 series, with which the DB4 line is often compared, had a more romantic cachet about it, even if it did use crude cart springs, almost bespoke electrics and had bodywork that might as well have been beaten out over a tree stump (a feature that applied to much Italian coachbuilding). The 250 was a Ferrari, after all, with everything that that implied, and, crudely made or not, a 1960s Ferrari holds together very well.

It is, however, not really fair to compare the two marques to this extent. There can be little doubt that Ferrari road cars were built in order to fund racing, specifically Formula 1, whereas the Aston Martin marque used racing to promote its road cars and, thereby, the wider interests of the David Brown Group. That this strategy was not always a resounding success reflects more on the racing machines than the road ones. Such was Brown's involvement with his other businesses that he only turned to single-seater racing, with a front-engined grand prix car, when the layout was already obsolescent.

The DB4GT remains a classic, as it aspired to and succeeded in the objective of being a road car that could be raced on the track with very little modification. It was almost Ferrari-like in its Italianate appearance, but other aspects of its character are thoroughly British; a very torquey engine and a build quality that was very hard to match. Its successor captured some of these qualities, but not all. However, in terms of the publicity that it was to

The DB4GT had an aggressive stance on the road, emphasised by the lack of bumpers.

The Bertone DB4GT 'Jet'

This car, Chassis 0201/L, was completed as a one-off in 1961 and shown at the Turin and Geneva Motor Shows. Unfortunately for Bertone, there was another car at Geneva that simply stopped the audience in its tracks. It was the E-Type Jaguar, the very existence of which put in doubt the wisdom of pursuing the DB4GT in any form, let alone with another package of exotic coachwork.

Bertone's DB4GT is an exceedingly pretty car, but I am not sure that it is any prettier than the Touring version and certainly does not stir the soul like the Zagato. Bertone had undertaken a not dissimilar exercise on an XK150 in 1958, and their DB4GT was very like it from the front, but much neater at the rear. The rear end of the XK effort had a definite Facel Vega look about it.

The Sanction 2 Zagatos

As students of the marque are well aware, there were mysterious production gaps in the DB4GT series, hard to account for now due to both the passage of time and appallingly sloppy record-keeping. The rebuilding and renumbering of wrecked chassis probably accounted for more than one of these; indeed, the famous 2VEV was totally rebuilt after an embarrassing prang.

A quick glance through the excellent Aston Martin Register reveals that chassis 0192, 0196, 0197 and 0198 were 'not built', and it was a hiatus that Aston Martin Chairman Victor Gauntlett was keen to fill. These were chassis numbers that straddled the production of the Project 214 cars, 0194 and 0195, technically at least. Further, the group of missing numbers was in the midst of a flurry of Zagato-bodied cars. Why not?

The heritage business was roaring along and the prices being paid for classic (or indeed any) Aston Martins were the

cause of much appreciative comment, within the trade at least. Several specialist engineers had also shortened DB4 chassis and made their own versions of the cars – which was only naughty (copyright aside) if they were to be passed off as originals, which none were – so Gauntlett and Peter Livanos deemed that the 'missing' cars should be built at last. The task of making the chassis fell to Richard Williams, the well-known specialist and custodian of the Aston Martin section of Gauntlett's personal car collection. By 1989 the chassis, carefully assembled from both rescued DB4 parts and brand-new metal, were ready.

Zagato had long since broken up the bucks for the shaping of the exquisite bodies, so Williams sent his own Zagato out to Milan to be used as a pattern. The results, when they came back, were startling. Effectively, Williams's own car had been 'cloned' to produce quadruplets, right down to the Aston Martin-Feltham chassis plates. Obviously the cars were not intended

to be 'original' in the sense that they could be substituted for the original 19 Zagato cars, but rather complement them. It was of course a relief that the exercise went so smoothly, and that there would now be a slightly wider audience for the world's prettiest car. Three of the cars used an interpretation of the triple bonnet bulge found on one of the early models, while another employed a more traditional bonnet air intake.

To drive, the Sanction 2 is marvellous. It is obviously a DB4; the Salisbury noises are there to remind you, lest you forget. The uprated engine is, at 4.2 litres, hugely powerful, probably in the region of 350bhp or so, breathing through three (noisy) 50mm Weber carburettors, which boost the top-end response almost off the clock. To rebuild any Marek straight-six engine to this specification is simply a matter of determination and cash, and it would transform any six-cylinder model from being merely a very fast car to an outrageous one. Utterly splendid.

A DB4GT Sanction 2 Zagato. No original Zagato had a bonnet quite like this, but you have to look closely to spot the difference.

The distinctive faired-in lamps of the
DB4GT, seen later on the Vantage
and the DB5.

generate, its shortcomings – and
there were very few – would be
forgiven by all but the very hard-
hearted.

Driving a DB4GT is not so very
different from a DB4: the steering is
sharper, courtesy of the shorter
chassis, and the engine much more
free-revving and eager in the upper
ranges, courtesy of the Weber
carburettors. I must confess that I
expected the springing to be harder.
The net effect of the lighter weight
and, as I consulted my records, a
deflection rate reduced from 132 to
110lb (60 to 50kg), makes the rear
end feel rather soft. Mind you, if you

The large, early bonnet scoop. As the
GT developed in parallel with the DB4,
changes were incorporated.

The GT interior: the narrow doors and lack of a rear seat can be compared to the standard offering.

whack in 40 gallons of fuel, which is the tank capacity, it would make a difference.

In standard form the GT is around 200lb (91kg) lighter than an early DB4, or just about 7 per cent, although many are lighter still; the power output is (roughly) 17 per cent more. When driving the car this obvious improvement is not clear (although it is smoother, courtesy of the twin plugs) until the engine starts to pull over about 4,000rpm. When this hidden power reserve suddenly appears, the effect is clear: the car squats on its compliant rear springs, tests the bump stops, and simply goes. The top-end acceleration is amazing by any standards, let alone those of a car that is nearly 40 years old. Having driven hotted DB4s, the effect is no surprise, but it is still immense fun. The same comment about tail lightness at speed applies, however.

Where the standard DB4 engine starts to fade away in terms of acceleration, the GT is still going strong. The doughty Bolster, driving a lightweight GT, managed to record 100mph (161kph) in 14.2 seconds, with 120 (193) coming up less than 7 seconds later. *Sports Car Graphic* were not quite so ambitious, with 0–100 in 18

Not much room for luggage.

seconds, but then Bolster was, shall we say, red-blooded, and perhaps Jerry Titus, the SCG tester, despite his own racing pedigree, had more respect for the gearbox. Bolster was changing into top at 115mph.

The upper architecture of the engine is clearly a major improvement, but not one that was entirely trouble-free at the time. Cracking between valve seats and spark plug apertures, for example, was a frequent problem, and keeping the twin-plug engine's two distributors on song (one is bad enough) was a very tiresome task. Again, bear in mind that GT cars of the late 1950s and early '60s were expected to be re-tuned at every major service. Until clever electronics arrived, this was simply one of life's realities. Some GTs even used magnetos, which, while clearly one of man's nobler creations, now require

their care and repair to reside in the hands of the specialist. To enjoy these cars today, the sensation comes complete with a whiff of hot oil, random misfires and a general feeling that this is all too good to last.

It is a shame in many ways that the Marek engine could not have benefited from modern techniques of engine management. The Weber system is about as good as carburettors get, and is sensitive enough to the engine's needs as any passive mechanical approach can be. No doubt someone has already looked at this matter (someone always does, if it's an Aston Martin), but it strikes me that in top tune this unit is so much nicer than a Jaguar that it almost seems a pity that the engine used in the DB7 is not Marek-inspired. On the other hand, perhaps it is. What a wonderful car.

The heart of the matter: the twin-ignition beWebered engine of the 4GT. Note the single nuts securing the camboxes.

The 'Project' cars

I defy anyone not to be moved by these. They are, basically, a subset of the DB4GT, although not all of them bear that out upon close scrutiny.

According to John Wyer, as related to Chris Nixon in the superb *Racing with the David Brown Aston Martins* (Transport Bookman, 1980), the pressure to return to endurance racing came, not from the works, but from the marque's dealers.

So it was that Project 212 came into being in early 1962. It was clearly a derivative of the DB4GT but used a Development project chassis number and a de Dion rear axle, which gave it extraordinary traction. Coupled with

The 'Project' cars had the misfortune to come up against fierce competition

the linered-out 3995cc DB4GT engine, it should have triumphed, particularly in the hands of drivers Graham Hill and Richie Ginther, but there were aerodynamic problems. Wyer also admitted that it was heavy, which was not a critical matter so far as endurance racing was concerned but still put a fair load on the engine. It retired on lap 79 of the 1962 Le Mans 24-hour race.

The three cars that followed for 1963, two Project 214 cars and a 215, were, in Wyer's words, 'much more serious'. They were variations upon a similar theme, but in all three cases they merely paid lip service to their heritage. They were pure racers and, while the 214 cars used (sneakily)

DB4GT chassis numbers, the 215 did not; the use of DB4GT chassis numbers was quite spurious, as the 214s owed nothing to their road-going cousins at all. The 214s reverted to 3.7-litre engines, while the 215 used a similar 3995cc block to the 212, but the car was much lighter. The cars were (and are) incredibly exciting to watch, but technology had overtaken them even before they were built.

A very nasty, and certainly very cynical, stunt was pulled over the fate of the second of the Project 214 cars. After the works effort closed down, largely triggered by John Wyer's departure to join the Ford GT40 project, several privateers had entered an assortment of cars for the classic races, and some of them received tacit works support. One such was Brian Hetreed, who entered the Nurburgring 1,000km race in 1964, driving DB4GT 0195. He had an awful crash, and died as a result of it.

AML asked his distraught widow what her instructions were concerning the wreck, once the dismal formalities had been taken care of, and they were quite explicit. Cut it up. Destroy it. Which they honourably did. In Britain. Despite our reverence for these machines, their manufacturers are no more sentimental about them than a farmer is about his beans. Besides which, it wasn't theirs. Nothing was kept.

When a racing car is scrapped after a mishap, particularly a fatal one, it ceases to exist. Its successes and failures are entered in the marque's log and that is that. It is a matter of profound regret when a driver is killed, of course, but the car is effectively cancelled. It may well be reconstructed by its maker, but superstition (always near the surface in motor racing) often prevents that.

Years later, in 1995, car 0195, complete with an elaborate 'legend', as John le Carré would have it, apparently came to light in a German scrapyard. Fantastically fortuitous. Imagine the lucky discoverer's surprise. Apparently, years of diligent effort had later uncovered a veritable treasure trove of original parts and triggered a lengthy search – a labour of love, really – for others, the most believable (and original) of which was a swatch of authentic, unused seating material that an ex-Newport Pagnell trimmer happened to have lying around. And, that, really, was about it. A DB4GT engine was installed, mated to a David Brown transmission, wrapped inside an admittedly nicely made reproduction chassis and body, all made with huge integrity and in the best possible taste. But the whole thing, however seductive, was basically rather disgusting. An historic racing car, ordered to be destroyed, rebuilt around one contemporary bit – in this case, part of an unused seat cushion. What will they think of next? Regrettably it happens all the time. It is surely DP001, the Dreadful Piltdown Special No 1.

A respected magazine, apparently without checking, wrote up the story, but even a cursory inspection of the known facts would have revealed that the thing was a clear, obvious, exploitative ringer. Personally, I really could not care less about originality; I take the view that the owner has the choice in the matter and that provided there is at least one example left, that will do for posterity. But when pure, cynical fakery becomes involved, I become as irate and wattling as any dodgy suede-shoed major at the RAC Club.

So, the Project cars marked the swansong of the works effort. They had the misfortune to come up

against a fierce assortment of competition: the Ferrari GTO, the lightweight Jaguar E-Types (them again), and, later of course, the next generation of racers as exemplified by the first manifestation of the incomparable Ford GT40, ironically with John Wyer at the helm. But by that time the factory had pulled out of racing again.

However, much was learned from them, as it always is in racing. The engines were fine, and the sheer power of them, well over 320bhp, managed to propel both the 214 and

215 down the Mulsanne Straight at Le Mans at 300kph (186mph). The modifications that were made to the rear end of these cars, to give them a Kamm tail, would find their way on to the DB6, so despite the ghastly episode at the Nurburgring, the evolution of the marque continued.

Project 215 very much at home at Goodwood.

Aston Martin
DB5

The DB5 popped out in the summer of 1963 with very little fanfare. Its arrival marked the end of the separate DB4 and the DB4GT; from now on there would be but one Aston Martin, and this was it. It was calculated to express the virtues of the DB4 and the GT in the way that the Vantage had, and, up to a point, it did.

The DB5 is a DB4 in all but name; it is, in effect, a sixth series, with some slightly more obvious improvements, notably in the engine and brake departments. Indeed, the original plans for the car denote it as a DB4 Series 6. Only the fact that there were

as many as 170 detailed modifications justified calling it a new model. A variation of the Girling system used on the DB5 had already been used on the DB4GT; the engine modifications were of a significantly lesser nature; and it had basically a 4-litre DB4 Special Series engine, with the later Vantage option of Weber carburettors being in line with at least the appearance of the GT engine, although lacking that car's twin ignition.

Moreover, the car's appearance also evoked the DB4GT. The faired-in headlamps, first seen in 1959 on the DB4GT and continued on the DB4 Vantage, were undeniably attractive, even if they detracted from night vision at high speed; the deemed rationale of the DB4GT was that of a

The frontal treatment of the DB4GT and the DB4 Vantage is carried through to the DB5. Later 5s had a chrome lamp fairing.

customer competition car, of limited production and infinite possibility and, up to a point, that was true, but the DB5 had no such pretensions.

Given the relatively large weight difference between the DB4GT and the DB5, totalling some 430lb (195kg), or almost 16 per cent of the dry weight of the 4GT, the claimed 325bhp output for the DB5 engine was basically necessary to attract the buyers. It was the first post-war model to sport a model badge declaring what it actually was, so it became a matter of some

The car is not always better for being easier to drive than its forebears

importance that the DB5 looked like a more powerful car than the final manifestation of the DB4. The fact that really it was nothing of the sort did little to deter buyers, however; the Goldfinger effect was as good an example of the role that global hype can play as anyone had ever seen. This was doubly ironic, since the DB5 that Sean Connery drove in that film was in fact a late DB4 Series 5, which, I think, rather proves the point of my earlier remark, that this car is not really a separate model at all. But the DB4 had achieved such a status by the end of its life that some improvement had to be made clear, hence the model badge.

This does not devalue it; it is a fine machine, even if the sensations created by driving and using it are somehow flabbier than those engendered by a properly sorted DB4 (let alone a GT). Its brakes are better for a start, and the engine, even if 282bhp for the SU-equipped version is a trifle optimistic, is, given its slightly over-square architecture, full of poke.

Aston Martin DB5
July 1963–September 1965

ENGINE:
In-line six-cylinders, alloy block and head
Bore x stroke   96 x 92mm
Capacity   3995cc
Valves   Twin ohc
Compression ratio   8.9:1
Carburettors   Three 2in SUs
Power   c280bhp at
                       5,500rpm

TRANSMISSION:
As DB4 Series 5, except five-speed ZF manual gearbox from chassis 1340. Borg Warner Model 8 automatic gearbox optional on later models, but few fitted

SUSPENSION:
Coil springs all round.
Front: Transverse wishbones, ball-jointed kingpins, anti-roll bar, Armstrong telescopic dampers
Back: Live axle, trailing arms, Watt linkage, Armstrong 'Selectaride' lever-arm dampers
Steering: Rack and pinion

BRAKES:
Girling discs all round

WHEELS:
6.70 x 15-inch

BODYWORK:
Bodywork and chassis as DB4 Series 5. Electric windows standard

LENGTH, WIDTH, WHEELBASE and HEIGHT: As DB4 Series 5

WEIGHT: 28.6cwt (1,453kg)

MAX SPEED: c140mph (225kph)

PRICE NEW: £4,250

DB5 VANTAGE:
As DB5 except:
Carburettors   Three Weber
                       45mm DCOE
Power   c310bhp at
                       5,500rpm

PRODUCTION FIGURES:
1,021

CHASSIS NUMBERS:
DB5C/1251 to DB5/2275
From chassis number:

1340 – ZF five-speed gearbox standardised

1526 – Electric cooling fan replaced by engine-driven one

1609 – 'DB5' badges fitted on bootlid and wings; engine compression raised to 8.9:1; carb jets modified; distributor upgraded; alternator control modified; Lucas charging indicator replaced; headlamp cowls now chromium-plated

Convertibles (still not Volantes) ran in four clutches: DB5C/1251–1300, 1501–1525, 1901–1925 and 2101–2123. A total of 123 convertibles were made (but see also the DB6 section)

A small run of 12 'Shooting brakes', converted from saloons and using saloon chassis numbers, was made by Harold Radford.

For Buying Hints, see Chapter 7.

The DB5 on the road.

It is torque, not merely bhp, that is the Holy Grail for the sports car. The DB5 has it – 40lb ft more than the DB4, if only 10lb ft more than the 4GT – and although it comes in later, the use of an overdrive top gear, as fitted to later ZF-equipped DB5s, allows the car to be driven with slightly more aplomb than its lighter predecessor. This is of course just the point – a car like this is not necessarily better, from the enthusiast's point of view, for being easier to drive.

If all you have ever driven is an MG or Triumph, or even a Big Healey, the DB5, like the DB4, is an experience. Although it is less involving than the 4, it is, in many ways, much more of a

piece than the earlier model, a logical and impressive evolution of it. The first fast car that I actually drove fast was a DB5 (I don't think my MGC counted and I couldn't trust the Rapide), and I do not think that I will ever forget it. I borrowed it while searching for an engine for the DB4. For me, DB Astons then became a personal litmus test of whether a car was really any good or not. Several, I should add, have passed that test with flying colours, despite the fact that I rather hoped that they would not.

From the rear the longer body is clear – compare it with the rear line of the DB4.

The DB5 was the last proper
Superleggera-built car.

Within the genre, the DB4 did best,
and I have stuck with them as a result.
By its appearance I had hoped that
the Maserati 3500 would stir me
somewhat, but it did not.

Gradually the DB5 became identified
with the marque in the same way that
the DB4 had done. It was certainly
really no quicker than a DB4: a
standing start quarter-mile in 16
seconds, a second slower than a DB4
Vantage, with 0–100mph (161kph) in
around 20 seconds, a full 3 seconds
more than the old car. Top speed was
similar, at around 140mph (225kph).
The Vantage version of the DB5 was a
different matter, but there is little
doubt that the standard car was
merely a heavier DB4.

As for its pretensions to the mantle of
the DB4GT, it was clear that the gap
had widened, even though the car was
more civilised – it had better silencing,
for example, although the running gear
was left alone, apart from a few
tweaks with castor angles, and the
spring rates and dampers remained
the same. It was, perhaps, a bit dull?

The DB5 drophead, as elegant
as the saloon.

The long-established Aston dashboard configuration looks almost austere when finished in the body colour, as on this DB5 convertible.

The introduction of a Vantage engine option at chassis 1763 went some way to recovering the performance lost. It is unlikely that the 314bhp quoted was anything near the real engine output, merely conveniently similar to the hottest DB4GT, but the performance pick-up was meaningful and, for the first time, the model was able to outstrip its predecessor. There was some modification to the camshaft profiles, and it was indeed mooted that what the engine really needed was twin ignition, but it never received it as a production feature. Nonetheless, in Vantage form the DB5 was once again a step forward as opposed to a great leap sideways. Our psychopath likes these cars: James Bond, innit?

From a driving point of view the DB5 Vantage is quieter than the DB4. The car I drove was equipped, like all DB5 Vantage models, with a five-speed ZF box, which perversely I did not like. Perhaps it was failing, but I found it noisier than the David Brown four-speed version. The bigger engine is instantly obvious, as are the three 45DCOE Weber carburettors; there was no airbox fitted so the noise was intrusive. The extra weight of the car over the shorter-bodied DB4 Series 4 is also evident, as cornering at speed is slightly more of an event than before.

In the intermediate gears, the car predictably comes into its own. The greater flexibility and higher torque of the bigger engine, coupled with closer ratios between second and third, at least provide more fun, even if not strictly necessary. The improvement over the standard four-speed DB5 that I drove years ago is clear, notwithstanding the fact that this car

The DB5 engine. The triple SUs of the Special Series DB4 are kept, but now it is 4 litres. Note the paired cambox nuts. This engine powered all Astons until the V8.

was in obviously better condition. As a Mr Toad *manqué* I would have preferred perhaps a little more noise. All in all it is a first-rate car, but perhaps not quite as chuckable as it could be. Perhaps the springs are not quite as hard as they should be for a car of this weight, or perhaps the Selectaride adjustable dampers are not quite as fit as they should be. Considering that the car weighs 340lb (154kg) more than a Series 4 DB4, it clearly needs more robust underpinning, for the back end feels relatively sloppy. Again, the tail is light at high speed.

There was, unsurprisingly, a convertible version of the DB5 and it broadly followed the approach taken when building the DB4, with extra bracing around the pelvis of the car to obviate the tendency of the body to flex, lacking as it does the upper Superleggera tubing. As you can imagine, however, the build technique militates against true rigidity when the roof is removed. It is not a critical matter, the Beach chassis being hugely

strong, so handling is not impaired in any way, but the alloy skin suffers: basically, it gets stretch marks. Compare this car to, say, a Porsche convertible and some of the benefits of light alloy bodywork underpinned by steel tube start to recede. The DB5 convertible is not a car for bad roads, although it is supremely elegant.

The last 37 DB5 chassis were employed as DB6 short-chassis Volantes.

The Vantage DB5 engine wears Weber carburettors.

The DB5 Radford estate cars

The Radford firm made 12 of these estates to special order, and they were hugely extravagant cars; in a sense they were manufactured twice, as fully finished DB5s went into their construction. Due to the nature of the Superleggera construction method (and its design) there was an unavoidable compromise in the conversion, which was that a DB5 saloon has a vast amount of strength at the rear, behind the screen, where the tubes converge with each other. The Radford conversion removed all of this, and as a result had to have a reinforcing steel frame inserted.

The cars are undeniably striking; the design, despite its use of clearly bought-in components, works well and the shape of the car is quite logical. The internal fittings are well carried out, and for the country gent who could afford it the Radford estate was a useful fashion accessory. Never mind that 'shooting brakes' often had to trek up to obscure moors in order to function; one assumes that a Land Rover would be available for such a task.

Aston Martin DB6

This is the model with the highest recognition factor of all the six-cylinder Astons. It is also one of the best. Whereas the DB5 was really only a variety of DB4, the DB6 veered away from that evolutionary path to a much greater degree than any other model thus far. Much of this was due to its method of construction, which used little of the Superleggera method, and more folded metal. It was no heavier, but it was stronger.

There are styling details from everywhere on the DB6, in particular the rear three-quarter windows, which recall the DB4GT Zagato, and the distinctive Kamm-inspired tail, harking back to the Project 214 racing cars. The front is pure DB5, apart from the oil cooler grille, and although the wheelbase is 4 inches (102mm) longer than the DB5, losing some visual proportion, the whole package has, in my view, an attraction of its own. The more you look, the better you get to like it, although a thorough inspection is required. The split bumpers not only save much weight, but are also elegant.

The DB6: this is a standard car of the first series, before lipped wheel arches and DBS wheels.

KGK 37D

Aston Martin DB6
Mark 1
October 1965–July 1969
Mark 2
July 1969–November 1970

ENGINE:
In-line six-cylinders, alloy block and head

Bore x stroke	96 x 92mm
Capacity	3995cc
Valves	Twin ohc
Compression ratio	8.9:1
Carburettors	Three 2in SUs
Power	c280bhp at 5,500rpm

TRANSMISSION:
As DB5

SUSPENSION:
Coil springs all round.
Front: Transverse wishbones, ball-jointed kingpins, anti-roll bar, Armstrong telescopic dampers
Back: Live axle, trailing arms, Watt linkage, Armstrong lever-arm dampers
Steering: Rack and pinion

BRAKES:
Girling discs all round

WHEELS:
6.70 x 15-inch

BODYWORK:
Four-seater, two-door body, hand-made in magnesium aluminium alloy, but no longer using Superleggera method. Kamm tail, longer and higher body than DB5. Volante convertible and five Radford-bodied estate cars offered. Chassis similar to DB5

LENGTH:	15ft 2in (4.62m)
WIDTH:	5ft 6in (1.67m)
WHEELBASE:	8ft 5in (2.66m)
HEIGHT:	4ft 6in (1.37m)
WEIGHT:	29.5cwt (1,498kg)
MAX SPEED:	c148mph (238kph)
PRICE NEW:	£5,000

400/V ENGINE (Vantage):
As 400 except:

Carburettors	Three 45mm Webers
Power	314bhp at 5,750rpm

400/SVC ENGINE (Vantage):
As 400/V except:

Compression ratio	9.4:1
Power	325bhp at 5,750rpm

400/FI ENGINE:
(optional fuel injection; 46 built)
As 400 except:

Compression ratio	9.4:1
Fuel system	AE Brico
Power	c300bhp at 5,750rpm

DB6 Mark 2:
As DB6 except:
Option of AE Brico fuel-injected engine (400/FI); 6J x 15-inch wheels; flared wheel arches; revised interior based on DBS model; modified rear suspension with air spring

PRODUCTION FIGURES:
DB6 Mark 1   1,327
Chassis numbers: DB6/2351/R to DB6/3599/LC and DB6/4001/R to DB6/4081

From chassis number:

2442 – Window weather strip replaced by extrusion

2990 (Vantage) – Laycock 10-inch clutch replaced by Borg & Beck 9½-inch

3186 – Laycock clutch replaces Borg & Beck on all saloons

3361 – Thermostat water return valve modified

3552 – Cranked gear lever fitted to RHD manual cars

4045 – Girling servo 11A replaced by 11B

4160 – Borg & Beck 9½-inch clutch replaced by 10½-inch

DB6 Mark 2   240
Chassis numbers: DB6Mk2/4101/R to DB6Mk2/4345/R

'Short chassis' Volante   37 cars built
Chassis numbers: DBVC/2301/LN to DBVC/2337/R

Mark 1 Volante   140 cars built
Chassis numbers: DBVC/3600/R–DBVC/3739/R

From chassis number:

3600 – Powered hood fitted

3601 – Laycock clutch replaced by Borg & Beck

Mk 2 Volante   38
Chassis numbers: DB6Mk2VC/3751/R to DB6Mk2VC/3788/L

Total DB6 production: 1,782

For Buying Hints, see Chapter 7.

The distinctive Kamm tail of the DB6 is its most obvious feature – but there are others – and it makes the DB6 one of the most stable Aston Martin six-cylinder cars, particularly at speeds over 120mph.

A common misconception is that the DB6 is a much heavier car than the DB5. It is not: the like-for-like differences account for a modest 18lb (8.2kg) of extra weight, so the DB6 owner pays no penalties for roomier accommodation and, it must be said, a much higher degree of straight-line stability. There are those who have discovered this, albeit late. There are, within AMOC circles, successful DB6 sprint and track cars; ten years ago, this would have been unthinkable. It is more than a shortage of DB4s that has caused this, for the DB6 has the rear suspension that the DB5 should have had: rear deflection rate is up from 132lb to 142 (60 to 64kg). Given that the DB5 was about 10 per cent heavier than the 4, and the DB6 is no heavier, this pays immediate benefits in the handling department, particularly because the DB6 has the best engine yet with which to start.

The main structural difference in the DB6 is seen under the skin of the car, with the discarding of the

Superleggera principle to define the contours of the body. The presence of the Superleggera badges on the bonnets of DB6s built until Touring's demise in 1967 is a confusing distraction, as the build method, which was carried over to the next model, and still in use today, is totally different. There is more alloy, but less steel. This also improves (or seems to) front/rear weight distribution. Perhaps the re-rated rear coils make a difference.

There are small differences inside, too. The seats underwent a redesign, not to everyone's taste, although I find them marginally more supportive, and of course there is a great deal more room. The DB6 is, eight years after the DB4, the car for the Aston Martin owner with kids.

Mechanically the DB6 shares its equipment with the DB5, with one or two improvements. In Vantage tune

The automatic is so awful that I wouldn't keep chickens in one

the engine was developed using exhaust cam profiles from the DB4GT. Together with revised jetting for the Webers and a later modification to the inlet cam, the Marek six-cylinder unit reached the apogee of its life with the DB6. Quoted power output from the Vantage, still at 4 litres, rose to 325bhp. It was not much more powerful than the DB5 had been at 314bhp, but, again, the difference makes itself felt when you drive it.

Unless, that is, you are unlucky enough to drive a DB6 with the Borg Warner Model 8 automatic transmission, which is unremittingly ghastly. A three-speed torque converter device, it was justifiably offered as a no-cost extra and is best avoided. It was also fitted to a handful of DB5s, most of which will have proper gearboxes by now. If one merely wishes to trundle about, it is, I suppose, fine; but be aware that the cost of buying, let alone installing, a five-speed ZF is not for the faint-hearted. I can come across no reference to a DB6 Vantage being thus fitted, but I am sure someone will turn one up.

So, an automatic DB6 looks the part, even sounds the part, and there are probably even further benefits in that it is extremely hard to red-line the engine. Even better, these cars will probably be of a lower mileage than

their manual cousins – they are so awful that wise owners will have taken the train. I would not keep chickens in one.

However, the performance figures of the DB6 in manual Vantage form are really quite extraordinary. The standing start quarter-mile and the 0–100mph (161kph) sprint are accomplished in 15 seconds or so, which is very much in DB4GT territory. It had taken Aston Martin three years to do it, but the numbers in the road tests were now firmly back where they should be.

The DB6 in profile. Unavoidably some balance is lost, but it has its own elegance.

The DB6 at rest.

When I drove a DB6 Mk I Vantage I frankly found it a much nicer car than I was expecting. It has much greater poise on bends than the 5 and is clearly more powerful. It is perhaps flattered by the fact that the 5 I drove was not fitted with a carburettor airbox, but the irritating noise from the DB6 front quarter-light (which simply will not seal properly) goes some way to even up the score.

The rear suspension works very well; the stronger springs and overhauled dampers instil a confidence that is all of a piece with the whole car. The limits of adhesion can be anticipated with much greater ease and the car behaves with great aplomb when the rear end finally gives up and slides. The longer wheelbase actually helps the handling over the earlier cars in a way that I did not anticipate at all; having been brought up to assume that the shorter the chassis the better the handling, I was pleasantly surprised that it is not always so.

Another revelation is the straight-line stability, due to the marked spoiler effect of the tail as well as the longer wheelbase. At 120mph (193kph), for example, a DB6 feels much more relaxed than any earlier six-cylinder Aston Martin road car, and there is no noticeable sensation of any lightness at the back. Finally, with the use of the race-developed Kamm tail, the car feels solid all the way up to twice the legal limit. For long journeys there is little doubt that the DB6 was the most practical six-cylinder proposition yet; the slightly awkward roofline is easily forgotten once you have driven it.

There was a further development of the DB6, which, after nearly calling it the DB7, was named the Mark 2. It was introduced in July 1969 and is easily identified by its lipped wheel arches, necessary to accommodate the wider wheels as fitted to the DBS model. Production overlapped with the latter until November 1970, when the last direct manifestation of the DB4 rolled out of the works at Newport Pagnell. By that time the DBS had been around for three years and had established itself very well indeed.

A fuel injection system, engineered by AE Brico, was offered on the Mark 2, and 46 were sold so equipped. It is rare to find them in original order today, as most have been converted to Weber carburation, but they are swift, since the fuel injection system demanded the higher-compression Vantage cylinder head.

The temptation to call the DB6 Mk 2 the DB7 was not as ephemeral a thing as is generally thought, as the project actually got as far as having badges made up for it. The DBS was, however, well in production and none but the most partisan could have described the Mark 2 as anything more than an updated model. It is the best of the DB6s, though, with improved handling and a nicely purposeful appearance.

As regards the convertible version, at last we can call it a Volante. There is a deal of nit-picking about what to call Aston Martin convertibles, but strictly speaking the name Volante (Italian for 'flying') only came in with the DB6.

There is a James Bond connection here, too. The bad egg in *Thunderball*

The DB6 engine is the best developed of them all.

The extra length of the DB6 chassis means that rear accommodation is acceptable, even on the Volante.

The DB6 Volante.

(1965) owned a boat that was apparently capable of as many improbable pyrotechnics as Bond's Aston Martin DB5, which made its second appearance in that film. The vessel was called the Disco Volante ('flying saucer'). There you are.

The first 37 DB6 Volante cars were actually built on DB5 chassis. Therefore they are, in my view, DB5s, given the structural differences between the 5 and the 6. It is a fine and supremely dull point, and not one upon which to dwell overlong, but those cars are the only DB6s to be built using Superleggera principles.

So, there are actually three groups of DB6 Volante: the DB5 cars, called 'short chassis', built between October 1965 and October 1966; the second group, retrospectively called Mark 1s, of which there were 140, in production from October 1966 to July 1969; and the third, the 38 Mark 2s, built from July 1969 to November 1970.

* * *

All these 'second-generation' cars are basically subsets of the DB4, so are variations upon a common theme. Like the DB Mark III, the DB6 is the most accomplished of the line, which is just as it should be. The early DB4s have a troublesome reputation, which was justified at the time, but very few cars will now be found with unrevised bearings or small sumps, which was the root of the problem.

The most beguiling of the group is probably the DB4, whereas the DB6 is certainly the most practical and also the nearest thing to a modern car in its appointments and general demeanour. It looks and feels as if it has 'lost the edge', as it were, but it hasn't, as a test drive will show.

The poor old Rapide is a worthy car, despite its critics and reputation. Rather like its later descendant, it is rather obvious, but as a quick four-door luxury saloon it really has few peers. And if it was a slow seller when new, its rate of progress from hand to hand now is positively glacial. It has its fans, though, which is pleasing.

The Mark 2 Volante has DBS seats and wheels.

The DB6 estate cars

Where the Radford DB5 'shooting brake' was a reasonable design success, the DB6 version was not. Again, the saloon car was used as a basis, but the rear-end architecture of the DB6, with its distinctive Kamm tail, sat very ill in the utility mode. I have a pet theory that the stylist of the immortal Austin Allegro (immortal only in the sense that the wretched things never quite seem to disappear) used the DB6 estate as his inspiration. Seven were made.

Aston Martin DBS

660 GGF

Just as Aston Martin got it right first time with the DB2 and the DB4, so they delivered the hat-trick with the DBS in 1967. It was clear that styling trends were veering away from the essentially 1950s influences that had created the two previous models. The DB6, the last of the DB4 line, was showing its age a little, and public perception was that the car was perhaps a step backwards from the DB4/5. (It wasn't, but a deep recession had hit sales anyway; the DB6 was always a slow seller when new, but for macroeconomic reasons rather than anything else. That fact has haunted it ever since, bizarrely.)

William Towns had been struggling on the fringes of automotive design for some time, messing about with door trims, handles and sundry minor details. After having joined Aston Martin as a seat designer (and a good one too – sit in a DBS to find that out), he had his chance to shine with

John Bolster with a DBS Vantage. The hotter engine, the best of the Marek 'sixes', was a no-cost option, but still some buyers declined it.

the DBS project. What he produced as a clay model went into production (more or less) unaltered, and the core shape was to remain the mainstay of the company for a quarter of a century until the introduction of the Virage.

Basically, the already massive DB6 chassis was widened by 4½ inches (114mm) – probably too much – and the wheelbase lengthened by 1 inch (25mm) to allow the repositioning of the engine rearwards. The body was,

Aesthetically the DBS was a pleasing accident

however, shorter than the DB6, so that the whole car was 1½ inches (38mm) shorter than its predecessor, but 6 inches (152mm) wider, at exactly 6 feet (1.83 metres). It was an impressive piece of design that paid homage to the past while anticipating the future. The DB4/5/6 grille was squared up, twin headlamps were used for the first time, and the front wings were peaked along their tops, a very Frank Feeley touch and rather reminiscent of the DB3S. Overall, the car looked squat, purposeful and massive – it was, weighing in at 31.25cwt (1589kg). It has been suggested that the original design of the DBS was intended to be a four-door saloon, a concept that actually took form as the Series 1 Lagonda V8, and if that is the case it goes some way towards explaining why the DBS is so wide, as if it was shortened but someone forgot to narrow it proportionally. Aesthetically, it was a pleasing accident.

Because the new V8 engine was not yet ready (see the next chapter), the 4-litre unit from the DB6 was fitted, in either standard or Vantage tune at no extra cost. In manual Vantage form it offered perfectly decent performance,

Aston Martin DBS
October 1967–May 1972

ENGINE:
In-line six-cylinders, alloy block and head

Bore x stroke	96 x 92mm
Capacity	3995cc
Valves	Twin ohc
Compression ratio	8.9:1
Carburettors	Three 2in SUs
Power	c280bhp at 5,500rpm

TRANSMISSION: As DB6

SUSPENSION:
Coil springs all round.
Front: Transverse wishbones, ball-jointed kingpins, anti-roll bar, Armstrong telescopic dampers
Back: de Dion axle, trailing links, Armstrong lever-arm dampers
Steering: Rack and pinion

BRAKES:
Girling discs all round, inboard at rear

WHEELS: 6J x 15-inch

BODYWORK:
New William Towns four-seater, two-door body, hand-built in alloy. Twin headlamps. Chassis similar to DB6, but wider

LENGTH:	15ft 1¼in (4.6m)
WIDTH:	6ft 0in (1.83m)
WHEELBASE:	8ft 6¾in (2.61m)
HEIGHT:	4ft 4in (1.32m)
WEIGHT:	31.25cwt (1,589kg)
MAX SPEED:	c142mph (228kph)
PRICE NEW:	£5,800

DBS AM Vantage
May 1972–July 1973

Vantage engine options available as for DB6. Otherwise as DBS, except twin headlamps replaced by single type, and grille modified

PRODUCTION FIGURES:
DBS   829
Chassis numbers: DBS 5001/R to DBS 5829/R
AM Vantage   71
Chassis numbers: AM/6001/R to AM/6070/R

The Touring DBS

In a sense, this was the swansong for the venerated Milan designer and builder. Relations were first-rate between Newport Pagnell and Touring, and this car (of which two were built) was exhibited at the 1966 London Motor Show. It relied heavily on the traditional construction methods that were a trademark of the firm and, indeed, hints of what was to come from the tiny Lamborghini company are clearly observable.

There were, however, problems with it. The car used a shortened DB6 floorpan and the engine was shifted 10½ inches (267mm) to the rear, which meant that the car could only be a two-seater; in fact, it was almost mid-engined. However well it handled, with almost perfect weight distribution, the bonnet aperture did not cover the engine. To remove the cylinder head, the whole engine had to come out, which was a slight oversight to say the least. In some ways it was a pity that the car never made it to volume production, but the DBS proper was on the way.

although perhaps not in the supercar league, managing 0–60mph (97kph) in around 7.5 seconds, with 100mph (161kph) coming up in around 18½ seconds. The top speed was just the right side of 140mph (225mph), a little quicker than the immortal DB4 and nothing to be sniffed at, given that it weighed the thick end of 400lb (182kg) more. But the DBS was just a little breathless at the same point that the DB4 was getting its second wind. (By the way, this car is never referred to as a DBS6 except by the cellular-phoned sheepskin-coated tendency. A DBS is already a six-cylinder model and nothing more need be said.)

The Harold Beach chassis finally acquired its de Dion rear end, which had been tried (and found wanting) on the Lagonda Rapide and sundry racers. It improved handling enormously, keeping the rear wheels upright and making the DBS the most sure-footed roadgoing Aston Martin yet. Huge width and heavy weight militate against the car being really chuckable, although obviously there is no harm in trying, providing you have the room. It can be made to drift well, however, on a suitably wide road.

Inside, the car is vast. Here, for the first time in an Aston, a family of four, providing they were affluent enough, could travel in real comfort, particularly if the optional air-

The frontal aspect of the DBS is, in my opinion, pleasingly pure. Others disagree, but it is what William Towns had in mind at the outset. Note the echo of the stepped grille that hints at the DB3S.

conditioning was fitted. All in all it is a very pleasant car, with few vices. The performance, although less robust than its precursors, is flattered by the car's sheer width and its staggering traction. After all, to find

For the first time a (wealthy) family of four could travel in real comfort

such a big car that would go this quickly was a rare thing. Today, of course, with the available engine uprating, the DBS can be transformed into a seriously fast car.

Whatever one feels about the car, it is undeniably handsome, and the

performance, with this best-developed version of the Marek six, is still very strong, sufficiently so that the massive improvement in rear grip over the previous models more than compensates for the poorer power-to-weight ratio. The de Dion layout is immensely reassuring: you feel safe in this car, and it is certainly quick enough for its size. There has been much criticism of the DBS, and much of it is unwarranted. I cannot agree with those who feel that it is not quick enough; is it perhaps more a case of its successor being – dare I say it – overpowered? Much underrated, extremely elegant and well worth a long look, if any car qualifies as 'a car for life', I think it is a close call between this and a DB4. One chum, who has an enviable stable of exotica, uses his as an everyday car.

For Buying Hints, see Chapter 15.

The DBS-derived Lagonda was created under the Brown regime, and a handful were sold during the Company Developments era; note how the grille is adapted from the regular AM V8 item.

Aston Martin
DBSV8

This is where it starts to get serious. The combination of Beach's altered chassis and Towns's styling had produced a brisk and handsome car, but not a startlingly fast one; the addition of Tadek Marek's V8 engine produced a machine so staggeringly powerful that few could believe it. Frankly, it is a car for grown-ups.

The specification of the Marek V8 is delicious: a four-cam V8, 85mm bore, 100mm stroke, capacity 5,340cc and red-lined at 6,200rpm. The main part of the engine, like its six-cylinder predecessor, is all-alloy and produced, in its early form, about 350bhp, with 400lb ft of torque. It is one of the greats, but it became so only after some trouble.

Marek had been working on a replacement for his straight-six engine for some time; it had appeared on the test bed in 1965 as a 4.8-litre V8, with the familiar four-cam valve layout. As the six-cylinder worked very well by this time, the build specification evolved logically into an all-alloy block with iron liners, and the capacity was edged out to 5 litres. Marek's nervousness about competition reappeared, but somewhat soothed by the success of the six-cylinder engine, he was happy to let his new engine power a pair of Lola T70s at the 1967 Le Mans.

There had been some thought of installing the V8 in a version of DP215, but it was clear by the time the engine was ready that the layout of the project cars had been made obsolete by the arrival of, among others, the

The rear deck of the early V8 follows the same treatment as the DBS.

Ford GT40 and its close relative the Lola T70. The two cars shared a common ancestry in many ways, as Eric Broadley, the Lola's designer, had made a great input into the Ford. Both cars, of course, were mid-engined.

Well, racing improves the breed, but only at the cost of some

Staggeringly powerful, this really is a car for grown-ups

embarrassment; the emphasis on lightness revealed that the structure of the block was simply not beefy enough, although the power output of the engine was not far short of 100bhp/litre, at more than 450bhp. Both Lolas failed early in the race, the loads imposed proving simply too much for the rather minimalist bottom-end castings.

This was rather awkward. The DBS, intended to accept the new V8, was scheduled to be launched at the London Motor Show in the October after Le Mans; obviously it could not happen, and was not destined to appear for another two years, but the intervening time was put to good use. Meanwhile the DBS chassis would easily accommodate the straight-six engine, but in this form the car was little more than a heavier but much better suspended DB6. It was a superb car in many ways, but some of the customers were fretting.

First the issue of the troublesome castings themselves, which were clearly a little skimpy, had to be addressed. In so doing it was realised that extra capacity could be built in at the same time, so the final dimensions of Marek's V8 were 85mm bore and 100mm stroke, offering a displacement of 5340cc; the power-to-weight ratio of the original engine itself, never mind the cars in which it

would be installed, was unheard of outside serious racing.

Not one to take risks where posterity (or warranty claims) were concerned, Marek's redesigned V8 was hugely strong; indeed, it has been taken out to 7 litres by private developers. Also bear in mind that this unit only weighed 30lb (13.6kg) more than the six-cylinder that it replaced. Marek had every reason to be pleased with his two years of development work, but there were still more hurdles to come.

It was the use of Bosch mechanical fuel injection (the same basic unit as used on the V8 Mercedes-Benz 600 engine) that gives these early cars their poor reputation. There is merit in

Aston Martin DBSV8 (Series 1 V8)
April 1970–May 1972

ENGINE:
V8, alloy block and heads

Bore x stroke	85 x 100mm
Capacity	5340cc
Valves	Twin ohc per bank
Compression ratio	9:1
Fuel system	Bosch mechanical fuel injection
Power	c325bhp at 5,000rpm

TRANSMISSION:
ZF five-speed manual or Chrysler Torqueflite three-speed automatic

SUSPENSION:
Coil springs all round.
Front: Unequal wishbones, anti-roll bar, Armstrong telescopic dampers
Back: de Dion axle, radius arms, trailing links, Armstrong 'Selectaride' lever-arm dampers
Steering: Adwest power-assisted rack and pinion

BRAKES:
Girling ventilated discs, inboard at rear

WHEELS:
Cast alloy, 7 x 15-inch

BODYWORK:
Bodywork and chassis as DBS

LENGTH:	15ft ½in (4.58m)
WIDTH:	6ft 0in (1.83m)
WHEELBASE:	8ft 6¾in (2.61m)
HEIGHT:	4ft 4¼in (1.33m)
WEIGHT (dry):	33.9cwt (1,725kg)
MAX SPEED:	160mph (257kph)
PRICE NEW:	£7,000

PRODUCTION FIGURES: 402
Chassis numbers: DBSV8/10001/R to DBSV8/10405/RCA

both defending and criticising it; on the debit side it is undeniably true that, without maintenance, the metering unit can leak fuel into the oil supply, dilute the lubricant and comprehensively wreck the bottom end; it is also true that, provided the system is set up correctly, it should be relatively trouble-free. Mercedes, for example, had little trouble with their own system, although the iron block of that car seldom heated up to the temperatures experienced by a cooking Aston Martin. The huge economic recession of the early 1970s put some of these cars into careless, or rather optimistic, hands as values

The manual will reach the motorway limit in second gear

collapsed, and there is no doubt that without the ritual 3,000-mile oil change, as well as regular maintenance of the fuel injection system, trouble is in store. And trouble, when it comes, is expensive.

A further point, that the car lacks low-rev torque, is also fair, but something with which one can easily live; it also makes the car reasonably easy to manage in slow traffic, although the engine tends to 'hunt' slightly at low revs. Once on the move, however, the grunt kicks in mightily, with 0–60mph (97kph) in a robust 6 seconds, 0–100 (161) in just over 14, and top speed a shade over 160mph (257kph), at which speed the engine is turning at a languid 6,000rpm. This was the sort of performance that was only enjoyed by sports racing cars barely a dozen years before. But the price to be paid is high: the fuel consumption of the V8 is staggering, as it is on the 6.3 Mercedes. Driven hard, or badly, the fuel-injected DBSV8 will deliver as little as 9 miles to the gallon, although 16–20 is more normal. A Rolls-Royce uses less fuel.

So, by the time the DBSV8 was sorted, it was clear to all that Aston Martin were back in the first rank of manufacturers, at least so far as the well-heeled were concerned. That they had indeed got it right first time around is fairly clear, as the DBSV8 was to last, with very little fundamental redesign, for a generation.

As a driving experience the DBSV8 is hugely fast. A manual version will reach the motorway legal limit in second gear, with nearly 100mph to come. Initially it is difficult to comprehend the sheer size of the car. At 6 feet (1.82 metres) wide it is, to say the least, roomy. Coupled with the vast power output, 345bhp or so, the prospect is intimidating. The low-speed response of the fuel injection is sluggish, but up into the middle ranges the car feels more comfortable and even appears to shrink. Unsurprisingly it seems rather similar to a DBS – merely a different noise. The car weighs around 300lb (136kg) more than a DBS, and the power output, estimated to be 345bhp at the works, provides acceleration and top speed of such an order that it becomes clear that the six-cylinder Vantage tune was nowhere near what was stated. *Motor* magazine, honourably taking the works at their word about the DBS power curve, estimated that the V8 must be producing 375bhp.

On an open road, any resemblance to its predecessor is firmly banished. Although the engine is only lightly stressed at 60bhp per litre, very much in line with other, lesser powerplants, the torque is quite simply electrifying above 4,000rpm. Below that, the engine feels a lot smaller than it really is. There is no doubt that the temptation to be totally stupid is right with you in the cockpit, a recurring theme with these cars.

But it is a most civilising experience, and it is something of a revelation that such a large car can both go and stop as well as handle. As one who was

schooled in the virtues of great cast-iron engines and vast amounts of unsprung weight, to me the DBSV8 is, for its size, an extraordinarily accomplished piece of kit. The de Dion rear end keeps the driving wheels firmly upright and the supple coil springs and massive dampers allow the car to be placed, despite its width, with great accuracy. Drifts are tempting, and reassuringly easy. The springing is hard enough, but the Armstrong Selectaride dampers will toughen it even more, (if they work), but never to the bone-shaking character of a racer. The limited-slip differential is reassuring but barely noticeable on the road. On the track it is another matter.

The most involving of these cars have the five-speed ZF gearbox; to a novice it seems necessary to change up constantly, as the engine spins to 5,000rpm with ridiculous ease. The Chrysler 'Torqueflite' automatic box is also marvellous and, designed as it was with big V8s in mind, is perfectly suited to the task. Aftermarket kits are available to lengthen the change period and perform the upward shifts at higher revs. Many have been so fitted, and the difference is marked.

Brakes are not up to modern standards, but are nonetheless well up to the task. The Girling ventilated discs, inboard at the rear, can have a tendency to overheat due to the temperatures in the rear axle, but only very hard driving will reveal this as the brake fluid edges up to boiling point. A further risk is that the brakes will heat up to the point where there is a serious risk of terminally degrading the adjacent differential oil seals. The results are two-fold: oil on the discs (bad) and rapid wear of the crown wheel and pinion (worse).

But if there is any doubt in the driver's mind of the old American adage that there is no substitute for cubic inches, then a quick spin in a well-sorted V8 will convince. But 'well-sorted' is the key here. The next chapter investigates some of the disadvantages of V8 ownership, but suffice to say that if the fuel injection is not set up properly the car can disappoint. As with some of its antecedents, however, modern improvements in oil technology have a marked effect on the whole engine, and measurable benefits on the reliability of the injector pump.

From the foregoing it is easy to gather that I am extremely partisan about these cars; I consider that an early manual V8 is as seminal a piece of work as a DB4 and is possessed not only of enough power to match a later Vantage, but also, like the DB4, a purity of line that later development did little to improve. Initially I found the specification of the car quite ridiculous (see the previous chapter). I had also been driven at great speed, but with no great skill, by the proud owner of one, and frankly I was scared witless. Do try one, though. Only a Jensen SP or a Mercedes 6.9 comes close in a straight line, but then, of course, there are corners to negotiate as well.

As events transpired, the Aston Martin V8 was to evolve into five separate phases. They were to remain the same car in essence, rather like the DB4, and again there was to be no separate designation of the various evolutions: they would either be DBSV8s or Aston Martin V8s. However, so strong was the identification of David Brown with the marque that the cars would continue to be called DBS long after he sold

the company, a trend that the current owners, Ford, have of course encouraged with the DB7.

* * *

Aston Martin had come a long way by the time Brown sold the company in 1972, and the cars being built reflected both the skills of the workforce and the simple difficulties of making such machines at anything that resembled a profit. Quite simply, the better the cars, the more money Brown lost on them.

For the person seeking ownership of one of these now, the choice in simple - V8 or straight-six? Again, the recent reputation of both cars belies their rare qualities. The DBS is quite simply magnificent, whether compared to a DB6 or a V8. It is not slow by any means, but the acceleration will not flatten the eyeballs either. It is a sophisticated and accomplished Grand Tourer and has a charm all its own.

The V8, by comparison, has hooligan genes. In automotive terms, however, there are few pleasures more satisfying as lighting up one of these, even an Ogle, I suppose, on a suitable road, perhaps the A286 running north from Chichester.

For Buying Hints, see Chapter 15.

In side profile, the car has attractive proportions. Close up, it is, however, very, very big.

Aston Martin
AMV8

A standard V8 is an enormously quick car – its size can catch out the unwary.

F or Aston Martin enthusiasts, who will always outnumber owners, 16 February 1972 was a black day. David Brown sold the firm to Company Developments Ltd, a minor-league Midlands-based asset-stripper, who were soon to realise that luxury car sales were a very sensitive bellwether of a fragile economy. The 1970s were just about to happen to Britain, with all that that implied. Forget the ghastly fashions and appalling TV – remember the oil shock, the stock market collapse, the three-day week, Ted Heath and the winter of discontent.

Given what was to happen 15 years later, the brief encounter between Henry Ford II and a small group of businessmen, which took place on the eve of the Company Developments takeover, is revealing. Ford had been approached by this small syndicate whose idea was that the Aston Martin marque should be bought by Ford, and the cars marketed in America with Ford engines and transmissions. It was the

The interior of a V8 is a new departure – luxury unseen since the Rapide.

re-emergence of the theme set by Carroll Shelby years before, and which had led to the Sunbeam Tiger, the AC Cobra and a host of imitators and might-have-beens. Ford said no, and Company Developments acquired Aston Martin.

It was a pity, really, for at least the Ford scheme had a business plan behind it that looked to car sales as

its mainspring as opposed to a situation that, when the dust settled, left the firm no better off, in receivership and minus assorted other assets. It does not get worse than that, really.

There were few differences between the DBSV8 and its successor, but the most significant one was probably the

Not quite lolling room, but the AM V8 still has reasonable rear accommodation.

The Ogle Aston Martins

An early visitor to Australia, whether a voluntary one or not we cannot be sure, after clapping his eyes upon a kangaroo is reported to have said, 'I don't ****ing believe it.' A similar reaction must surely have been generated at the Montreal show of January 1972.

These Ogles are technically specials, thank heaven, and are included only as an example of what can happen when designers go completely Tonto. Before I inspected one closely, I had assumed that the vilest excesses of the 1970s were no worse than flared trousers or Jason King. No. This was. If you think it amazing that even one

was built, then marvel at the staggering fact that two were, then swoon at the news that someone actually made a replica.

It is, underneath its superficial ghastliness, a DBSV8. I will never understand how, when the current catalogue model in the Aston Martin range was the delicious Towns-styled DBS, the Ogle design company could come up with this. But then again, they had done it before, and they would do it again. What an utterly frightful confection. Irritatingly, it goes rather better than a standard car, being lighter and having a better weight distribution.

Significantly, the Ogle was introduced at the very top of the stock market cycle, just before the major collapse that was to put Aston Martin into receivership (again). If they do another one, investors be warned.

The Ogle Aston Martin did drive well, but was hardly an improvement visually.

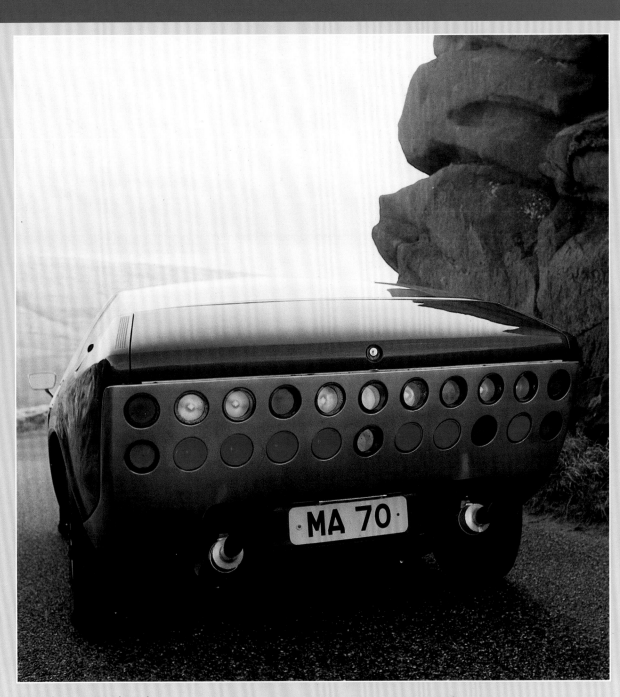

The Ogle's sequential rear lamps
were a novelty.

The early fuel-injected V8, in this case fitted in an Ogle car.

price. From a shade under £7,000, the new AMV8, as it was called, was now a cool £9,000. It was probably a fairer price to charge, but it was still an eye-watering price increase for those owners who were trying to justify buying a new car (or even trying hard to hold on to their old one) in the face of economic stagnation and a stock market in the grip of a nervous collapse. This, of course was even before the oil price rise.

When that happened sales, of course, imploded and the bean-counters moved in, redundancies and economies were made, and as a

Sales dropped, cuts were made, and the quality control weakened

result the quality control side of the business, always a source of pride to the firm, weakened rapidly. The clear lack of capital in the face of a sales crisis put AML Ltd between a rock and a hard place. The sports ground (which was one of the assets due for stripping anyway) was sold hurriedly at a knockdown price to defray borrowings, but this of course did nothing for the quality of the cars. Within a year of the sale by David Brown, the firm was in the throes of a major crisis.

This was important in two ways. First, the oil shock had a direct effect on the marque. Second, the fallout from the financial crash meant that second-hand prices for Aston Martins plummeted and many fell into the hands of those who could not, or would not, maintain them properly. When oil changes are missed, servicing is skimped and cheap

substitute parts are used, it does not take long for a beautiful, agile and powerful car to turn into a smoke-belching clunker. Add a few nasty blow-over paint jobs and the net result is that an Aston Martin from the early 1970s could easily be a nightmare to own and run, as the accompanying 'Buying Hints' explain. Naturally this also applies to anything else in the same league, but few of them have hand-built engines or hand-formed bodywork.

Having said all that, it is also the case that the vast increase in values that was ushered in by the 1980s also triggered some heavy expenditure on restoration; the flight away from

financial assets in the wake of the 1987 stock market crash had the same effect on classic cars as it did on property – there was a spike upwards in values of anything with a remotely historic pedigree, and Aston Martins were some of the biggest gainers, as the earlier anecdote about my briefly owned DB Mark III illustrates.

To be fair to Company Developments, they were not entirely paralysed by the crisis. Their attempt to re-introduce the Lagonda marque, on the same basis as the Rapide, by stretching a V8 chassis and rebodying it, was not a success, but it was at least something, even if it smacked of

An Aston Martin V8 engine is an imposing sight, and is as strong as it looks.

boardroom panic. David Brown had done it, after all. It had all the elegance of the 2+2 Jaguar E-Type, which is to say not a lot. Five more were made, and, for what they are, they are nice cars, but the crisis that was gripping Aston Martin, which had started as the inevitable result of cheeseparing and uncertainty, was to develop into a full-blown catastrophe before long.

Aston Martin
AM Vantage

The inclusion of an 'entry level' Aston Martin, with the well-tried six-cylinder Marek engine, merely reflected the swingeing price increases that Company Developments had sought for the flagship V8. The price of the AM Vantage was, in fact, within a few pounds of the original V8-engined DBS before the company changed hands. The engine was the same as that fitted to the last of the DBS cars, and the body was as for the then

The six-cylinder Vantage attempted to steel the thunder of Aston Martin's highly-tuned road car reputation. As such it failed. (Aston Martin Lagonda)

current Aston Martin V8 model, with single headlights but wire wheels. It was neither fish nor fowl, really, and something of a marketing setback.

However, in its defence it was the best of the Marek 'sixes', and despite the fact that the car that it powered had no soul – the unwanted child, as it were – it is a physical manifestation of the best of the firm in the 1960s. It was right, it worked, it was powerful, but it was a mistake. The use of the Vantage designation was probably also a mistake. Heretofore the Vantage appellation had always implied a 'hotter' version of an existing car, rather than a type in

itself, and it was clear, because no one denied it, that the powerplant of the car was basically 15 years old and, sentiment aside, was in all ways inferior to the V8 engine of the standard model.

Thus the AM Vantage was a decent enough car, no better than the DBS (and quite possibly a little worse, given the stringent economies being imposed at Newport Pagnell), but to a prospective owner of a V8 costing £2,000 more, it was a small slap in the face. The 'we've got them, you want them' attitude sat ill with the times, which were getting tougher weekly. Die-hards would have

preferred a DB6 continuation, for there can be little doubt that the AM Vantage was, in PR terms, something of an exploding cigar. So, the V8 engine is worth £2,000, is it? Right you are, I'll buy a Jensen. Or a Jaguar. This, in many cases, is exactly what happened. People got cross.

It was a pity, really. But do bear in mind, in case this all sounds unfair, that the rate of inflation in the 1970s was starting to accelerate exponentially as a result of easy credit – the idea of manufacturers calmly marking up their products by 20 per cent nowadays seems laughable outside Russia, but in Britain it was a commonplace practice. Bear in mind also that the plight of Company Developments was a serious one: they had to contend with both a shrinking market and high fixed costs, with little ability to be flexible in their approach to manufacture. They had misunderstood a basic tenet of what it was they now did, which was to make superior motor cars for a discerning and fastidious customer base. But if the customers thought that the product was not up to snuff, they would not buy it. Gaps in the company's planning left them critically short of precious capital when the going got tough. And it got very tough indeed.

The new owners of Aston Martin were not only naïve if they thought that this model would fit into a stopgap marketing strategy; they were also starting to run scared. As the stock market headed to the levels last seen at the time of Dunkirk, it became clear that their plans, like those of many others, were not surviving their first contact with reality. As value was rapidly stripped from an inflation-stricken UK economy, their own position was starting to become questionable, which is the first stage of fiscally untenable. Their business plan was denuded of credibility as sales forecasts, compounded by the kind of reactive marketing that gave

the world the AM Vantage, proved themselves to be eerily inaccurate, as did those of many other people.

Seventy AM Vantage cars were sold, and, searching the back numbers of various magazines, I have been unable to report that anyone actually road tested one. They need not have bothered anyway; due to its technical specification being identical to that of a DBS Vantage, the AM is to all intents the same car.

It taught a valuable lesson to everyone. Aston Martin is not a trifler's marque; as soon as anyone strays towards hinting that it might be, the magic is lost. Not that the price was in any way trifling, but it led many buyers to question the achievement-driven integrity of the firm now that it was no longer part of the David Brown corporation. They were right. It was not working, and by the end of 1974 production of all models was cut back and the company was put into receivership.

The response to the news was extraordinary; locally, of course, with so many people depending upon Aston Martin for business, directly or not, there was gloom tinged with fatalism. There were apparently thoughts of a Government rescue, but they failed to reach serious consideration in the cabinet – no concern with a hint of the bloated plutocrat about it would be eligible for a bail-out. Leyland famously received aid, as did the Triumph motorcycle co-operative at Meriden and many others, but neither Aston Martin nor Jensen Motors saw any.

Schoolchildren (mainly boys, but records are inexact) sent their savings, and the Goldfinger generation responded with a 'something must be done' outcry, but it was to be six months before a qualified buyer was found. Sundry deal-makers drifted in and out, as they always do in receiverships, but nothing happened until the summer

of 1975, and then only as a result of serendipity.

Six months is an agonisingly long time in a receivership; all the uncertainties, the time-wasting, the lay-offs, the erosion of skills, the defections, the simple needs of survival of the workforce, all take their toll. In Newport Pagnell's case many staff opted to carry on working for reduced or no wages. At the skilled craft level, all were acutely aware that the vital factory floor synergy that had developed organically was basic to the company's product and that, if it were to survive, compromises, many of them personal, all of them financial, would have to be made. It has been suggested that it was this attitude, this deeply unfashionable solidarity of the unionised workers with their toffs' product, that went a long way to dooming the prospect of Aston Martin ever being in receipt of Government cash. On the other hand, that may just be a lack of charity on my part.

The morale of the workforce, who were as dependent upon the firm as the firm was upon them, plunged to new lows as the receivership dragged on. The anguish in Newport Pagnell was real, and there was a genuine fear that as the crisis ground on, the status quo could never be recovered. The coachbuilders, engine-builders, trimmers and other precious specialists suddenly found that they had no value, and the quality of the economic downturn was so savage that there was serious doubt at many levels as to whether there would ever be any recovery. In fact, the worst was already over, but it did not appear so to the traumatised workforce, or indeed to the Government.

All this commitment may have cut no ice with Tony Benn, the new Government minister concerned, but it did trigger some positive responses elsewhere. Peter Sprague, an

American, and George Minden, a Canadian, managed to stop the rot in so far as the receivers would not, in exchange for a consideration, liquidate the assets of the company. Others followed. Alan Curtis, a property developer (one of few who had survived, and who had been an Aston Martin owner and even contemplated bidding for the whole company) and Denis Flather (a retired businessman who had raced

It took a year to rebuild production momentum – but the new owners had a bold plan

Lagondas before the war) also joined in the consortium shortly afterwards. The firm was saved, for the moment, as Aston Martin Lagonda (1975) Ltd, but was severely depleted by the cruel arithmetic of insolvency. It was to take the firm a year to sort itself out, to rebuild momentum in terms of production, yet the new owners would hatch a bold plan – one that combined both first principles and established thinking. They were, within 14 months, to produce an entirely new model.

Buying Hints: DBS, DBSV8, AMV8 & Vantage

Given that many people's negative Aston experiences stem from acquaintance with badly maintained cars from the 1970s, this is a good place to run through some of the more serious pitfalls of V8 ownership.

1. As on all Astons, the state of the chassis is critical. Look for rot in the sills, the pedal box and the rear suspension mounts, coupled with signs of electrolytic corrosion damage where steel meets alloy. Blocked drainage holes can cause water to gather in door bottoms and the boot. Likewise, if the car has a sunroof the drain tubes can clog. Corrosion can often be seen under the fuel fillers. The under-bonnet area is less prone to this for the simple reason that the vast heat soak from the alloy engine causes swift evaporation of fluids. Given the cost (and risks) of alloy welding, an obviously corroded car is best avoided.

2. Normal places to look for accident damage are the front cradle, which supports the engine and carries the suspension and steering, together with the extremes of the bodywork. Paint repairs are not always easy to identify, and the car should be inspected from an oblique angle, outside on a clear day rather than cheek by jowl in a crowded showroom. Check for consistency in panel shut lines and an even stance.

3. The V8 engine is sturdy if well-maintained; six-figure mileages are not uncommon with no major work, but like all alloy engines the unit requires regular oil changes. The differences between the coefficients of expansion of alloy, iron and steel (something of a theme with Aston Martins of all ages) can change bearing gaps very quickly, with bearing failure a distinct risk on poorly maintained engines. Therefore oil pressure is as important to the engine as rust or damage is to the chassis, so observe it closely. It is lower than that found in the Marek 'six', but still needs

to be high to preserve bearing life.

4. While on the subject of lubrication, although the specific output of the engine is mild, it is still a mighty device and prone to abuse. Engines from automatic cars tend to last a little longer, as over-revving is less likely. Overheating of an alloy engine is no trivial matter, and head gasket failure on the V8 is by no means rare, although it can be frustratingly hard to detect without specialist equipment.

5. The bottom end of the V8 engine can offer some puzzles; it is not unknown for crankshaft plugs to loosen in early engines, for example, causing volatile oil pressure.

6. Automatic boxes are Chrysler and usually reliable, but check for burned fluid. The five-speed ZF unit can be noisy, and, although it will seldom fail, clutch wear can be high.

7. A weak spot on the V8 is the differential; the use of inboard brakes heats up the unit greatly and thins the transmission oil, allowing it to beat the seals, with the result that the brake discs can be wetted by it. The seals themselves can also degrade as a result of the heat, which compounds the

problem. One can imagine the effect of a differential giving out at high speed. This is the single potential problem that needs to be checked; it is expensive to rectify given the labour involved.

8. The trim, being hand-made, is simple, if costly, to restore.

Bespoke performance costs money, and while there are always good cars around, there are also plenty that look very tempting but are in fact restoration projects waiting to happen.

If your chosen example is generally tired, it needs to have at least a decent chassis and body to justify buying it. If it is a bit rusty, with a tired interior, grotty paint and a vague service history, it should be cheap. Bear in mind, however, that the abolition of leaded petrol will mandate a top-end overhaul to replace valve guides and seats anyway, so their state is of less concern.

The Volante is no more tricky than any other model, but the hood should be closely checked as repairs are costly.

A V8 under full restoration. The spares support for these cars is splendid.

Aston Martin *Lagonda*

S prague, Minden, Curtis and Flather were all in place by the autumn of 1975. At the end of the year, Curtis and Flather became directors and as the winter of 1976 ended, thoughts turned to the possibility of a new car. William Towns had drawn up some sketches and the board were unanimous that the car would cause a sensation. It would use a V8 chassis but, unlike the 'stretched' Lagonda that had been built during the Company

Developments period (AML 1975 built two more of them), this would have a body design all its own.

The Lagonda marque only played a walk-on part in the development of the Aston Martin story; it never really recovered its pre-war role as a Grand Touring car and, while the post-war Lagondas were worthy vehicles, they were rather uninspiring. The Rapide of 1961 was a superb car in many ways but risibly expensive, serving

The Aston Martin Lagonda has the highest recognition factor of any marque in the world.

The early digital read-outs were groundbreaking in their cleverness, but costly.

mainly to keep everyone's eye off the ball and stretch resources. The Lagonda that accompanied the AMV8 was just a stretched Aston Martin and visually rather dodgy, so the track record of the marque, at least domestically, was patchy.

So the decision to modify the V8 chassis and redesign the whole vehicle to produce a brand new model was a brave one. One reason for it was the hope of developing a decent export market to the newly rich Middle East, and to a large degree that was accomplished. In

terms of naming it, it was decided to call it simply the Aston Martin Lagonda – it was felt that the use of Lagonda as a model name rather than a marque name might in fact lead to a renaissance of the marque. It almost did.

In design terms the Lagonda was – is – leading edge. The design went from paper to metal in eight months, and in October 1976 the new car broke cover at the London Motor Show and heads turned. Since the economy had seemed to turn on a sixpence after the panic of the 1974 stock market

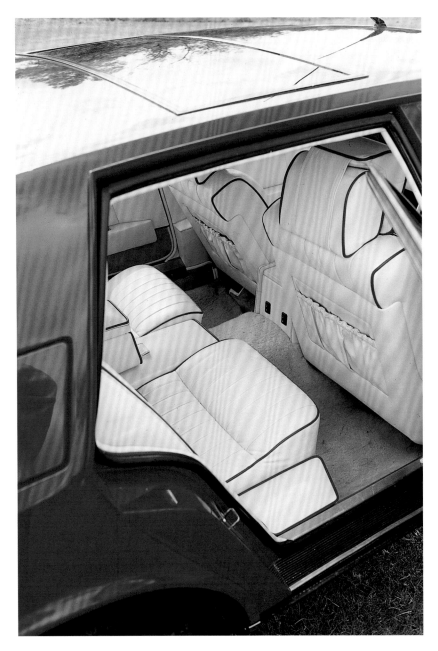

The rear cabin of the Lagonda. It is surprisingly compact, although beautifully made.

dashboard, the first that had ever been produced. To all concerned outside Newport Pagnell, the car seemed as modern as tomorrow.

The Aston Martin Lagonda is a splendid car. The traditionalists have it that it is garish and showy, but to an extent that was the whole point. There has seldom been a vehicle that captivated the media as this one did. The fact that one of the first sold (which did not actually work) was bought by the Marchioness of Tavistock (on her credit card, as an anniversary present for her husband) had tabloid Fleet Street in a complete swoon. (The reality was rather different: the Marchioness was actually a design director of Aston Martin and the whole episode was pure spin, even down to the pleased collusion of the credit card firm.)

All at once, though, the Lagonda was the new toff's car. If the six-cylinder AM Vantage had been a limp, cynical makeweight, born out of desperation, the new management's Aston Martin Lagonda proved that the patience of the receiver had been totally justified, for all agreed that it was both beautifully made and visually striking, even if it was full of bugs.

The car did not actually commence production until April 1978 and the list price started to rise fast. By 1979 it was to have doubled.

Over in America, Rex Woodgate, the President of AML Inc, was breathing a deep sigh of relief at the way things were going. He had struggled with the fast-changing emission laws that were sweeping the United States as well as fretting over the financial state of the company. It was he who had been the first point of contact for Peter Sprague, who had put the successful consortium together to buy the firm out of receivership.

Woodgate was also an engineer. Before joining Aston Martin in 1954 he had worked with the immortal Alf

crash, the new car almost embodied a new confidence, a craving for extravagance.

The V8 chassis had been stretched a foot to accommodate the passengers in comfort. Mike Loasby, the Chief Engineer, altered the suspension and steering settings to produce a firm but compliant ride, and Towns's coachwork sat very well on it. A key feature of the interior was a digital

Francis at HWM in the early post-war racing days, and therefore knew his way around an engine. It was he who had, on a shoestring budget, organised the first turbocharged V8, initially as a way round the emission regulations. It was a success, but ultimately did not need to go into production as Woodgate finally managed to homologate the existing carburettor cars for sale in America in 1975. After a three-year period of flat sales, between 1971 and 1975 AML managed to exist more or less purely on the basis of servicing and spares.

But the work was done, and when the question of making a faster Lagonda came up it was to turbocharging that Aston Martin turned, installing such equipment in a roadgoing Lagonda in late 1979. The engine produced astonishing low-end grunt: 500lb ft of torque at 3,500rpm. Although the engine used carburettors, it was a blueprint for the most outrageous

Aston Martin yet, which was at that time undergoing development.

The Lagonda has such a visual impact, is so obviously exactly what it is, that even today the driver of one

For a time AML Inc. survived on servicing and spares

feels conspicuous, even nervous, in a way that would be impossible in, say, a four-door Bentley. As happened during the 1970s, when values crashed, several have fallen into the hands of our cheery psychopath, who bangs them out for what he can get, establishing a clearing price that is suspiciously low. A friend of mine

from the Middle East, who as a child saw a Lagonda in Kuwait when it was new, was completely smitten by it, and when I flipped open a car comic and showed him the classified ads, he was outraged that the cars were so cheap. He didn't buy one, though. There is a moral in there somewhere.

The Lagonda deserves better than this. It was a brave decision to make it, it was an excellent car when it appeared, one that captivated the whole country, and those who have owned them have, by and large, liked them. It did a lot of good for Aston Martin, too.

The Lagonda badge – this was the last production car to wear it.

Development
of the V8 saloon

The AMOC have defined five separate phases in the life of the V8 saloon, but they are really only iterations upon a common theme. Obviously the DBSV8 is, historically at least, a model of its own and the second variant is the first AMV8. For those new to the marque, it becomes a little complicated from then on, so this chapter will attempt to tease out some of the distinguishing features. The cars are either DBSV8s or AMV8s in the classified ads, so perhaps a brief vade-mecum is a good idea.

The switch from twin headlamps to single ones is a distinctive feature with the AMV8, as is the shallower grille. The body is actually 2½ inches (64mm) longer than the DBS and there is more room in the boot, but that is about it, visually. The engine, complete with its fuel injection, remained unchanged. The 3.33:1 manual transmission final drive was standardised, as was the 2.88:1 for the automatic model. This 'series 2' marked the basis for the development of all V8 saloons, which were to be produced until 1989. Confusingly, some will be found wearing David Brown Aston Martin badges – there were simply some left in the bin, a simple and understandable economy, and one that may also reflect a certain wistfulness on the part of some of the production staff. It would, I think, be nice to think so.

The Bosch fuel injection was proving a little unpopular, both for reasons of fuel economy and low-end

smoothness. Accordingly in August 1973 it was deleted and replaced by four twin-choke down-draught Weber carburettors. In many ways this could be seen as a technical step backwards, but it really only reflected the state of development of fuel injection systems outside the diesel business. This 'series 3' car was basically very similar to the previous one, although it grew three-quarters of an inch, and there were several detailed modifications in terms of material used for insulation and so forth. The most obvious feature is the increased height of the bonnet scoop, necessary to clear the intakes of the huge carburettors. It is an unattractive feature in my view, but obviously necessary. The result is a better car all round, but a small amount of top-end grunt has been sacrificed for a more consistent power curve and undoubtedly smoother progress.

These were, and are, amazingly rapid cars, and there was some well-founded concern that, elegant though Towns's design was, there was an element of rear-end lift at speed. The response to this was 1978's Oscar India (Air Traffic Control-speak for 'OI', which represented nothing more exotic than 'October Introduction'). This car received a facelift both inside and out; the most obvious external signs were a lipped spoiler on the boot and a blanked-off power bulge on the bonnet.

In the cabin, the air-conditioning was improved, and the headlining was

now made of leather, which was an exotic touch. If you agree that the single-headlight models are visually acceptable over Towns's original design, then possibly the 'series 4' Oscar India car is the one for you. It has carburettors, a feature that satisfies the Luddite always present in British car enthusiasts, and an interior that triggers an instant sense of smugness.

Ultimately, in January 1986, the technology of fuel injection caught up with the needs of Marek's splendid engine, when the final version of the V8 saloon was unveiled at the New York Motor Show. Lo and behold, it

Some top end grunt has been sacrificed for smoother power

had a flat bonnet, reflecting the use of Weber/Marelli fuel injection. The quoted power of the engine was 305bhp, which can hardly be considered as much progress over the original version, but elsewhere work had been done that really did count as progress.

If one stands at the wrong end of the telescope, as it were, and tries to identify the point at which the Aston Martin V8 stopped being a benchmark of low-key understatement for quality and performance, and something of a

The Bulldog

Few cars in that small and slightly speculative universe of one-offs and prototypes ever see the light of day as production models and that is often a blessing. Such 'Concept Cars' are inevitably extravagant and more often than not designed to generate a reaction more visceral than a mere sketch or styling model ever can. This is such a car.

It was the acclaim that greeted the AM Lagonda that persuaded AML that they could push the boundaries of credibility even further than they already had. Accordingly, Mike Loasby, who had done so much development work on the Lagonda, undertook a new project, which became DPK901. He took over a small building at Cranfield and set to work. No one denied the rumour that the undertaking had something to do with a sketch produced by William Towns, but Loasby resigned soon afterwards to go and work for John DeLorean. The project was taken into

the works under the wing of Steve Coughlin (Loasby's successor), Keith Martin and Steve Hallam.

By the autumn of 1979 the car was more or less ready and, when shown to the press in the spring of 1980, caused a bigger sensation than the Lagonda ever had. It was christened 'Bulldog'.

It was not short of gadgetry, the Bulldog. It was the classic Towns wedge shape, but fitted with huge gull-wing doors, four separate fuel tanks and fireproofed bulkheads. A vast windscreen was specially commissioned from Pilkington, swept by a single wiper over 2 feet (600mm) long. Instrumentation was of the fibre-optic, liquid-crystal type as developed for the Lagonda and, most significantly, the engine was in the back.

The car would, it was hoped, achieve 200mph (322kph). Looking at the

specification of the engine, it was very tempting to think so. It was another use of forced induction, which was becoming a minor fetish at Newport Pagnell at the time. Rather than follow the Lagonda route, the engine reverted to the Bosch fuel injection of the DBSV8 with the addition of two Garrett turbochargers; power was 600bhp at 6,000rpm.

It never did get up to 200mph, however. Technical delays with the engine (they eventually liberated 700bhp) and huge aerodynamic lift problems prevented it, but later, at the end of 1980, 191mph (307kph) was achieved at MIRA.

The Bulldog. DP K9, this extravagant creation was not, perhaps wisely, put into production, but served as a test bed for the hugely powerful turbocharged Marek V8. (Aston Martin Lagonda)

The built-in spoiler was introduced with the 'Oscar India' type.

cypher for bags of swank, opinions differ markedly. Some say that the acme of the type is best expressed by the original model, warts and all under the bonnet, but blessed by William Towns's stunningly simple package of balance, line and spatial economy. Others prefer the last of the line, the 'PoW spec Volante' (a phrase beloved of the sheepskin-coat-and-mobile-phone tendency which describes cars similar to the one owned by Prince Charles), bespoilered, skirted and wearing extremely complicated wheels and surprising colours. No prizes for guessing my view – but what of the marketplace?

Aston sales, fuelled by the economic recovery and at last an adequate capital base, strengthened. There is no doubt that despite the questionable visuals of the last V8 models, they were very quick. They were also more or less bug-free, given the development time available to perfect Marek's original sound core V8 design. As the model matured it became faster and smoother, just as it should.

But are they nice cars? The fact that they sold well in the 1980s, when I was religiously push-starting my DB4 Vantage every day (broken solenoid) and cursing the day I first met Mr Goldstone, and every other car flashing past seemed to be either German or a V8, suggests that they were a success and, commercially at least, they were. Owners I spoke to (they often stopped to assist) seemed pleased.

But 'nice' does not quite do it. The later cars are also incredibly dated now; the view hinted at above, that the first one was the best one, holds up very well when you survey a late '80s V8 Volante alongside, say, a Virage, a new Porsche or a Series 1 DBSV8. It is clearly a 1960s design

Aston Martin V8 production changes

Series 2
April 1972–August 1973
From chassis number:

V810501 - Cam covers now marked 'Aston Martin Lagonda'; twin quartz headlamps replace previous paired layout; radiator grille modified to accommodate; body length increased to 15ft 3in; spare wheel now stowed flat; transistorised ignition fitted; engine bulkhead insulation improved; air box modified; axle ratios 3.33:1 (manual) and 2.88:1 (automatic) standardised; steering wheel now leather-covered.

PRICE NEW: £9,000

Series 3
(contemporary with Series 1 Vantage)
August 1973–October 1978
From chassis number:

V811002 - Fuel injection replaced by four twin-choke Weber carburettors; water, oil and transmission cooling all upgraded; bonnet bulge deepened and lengthened; ventilation louvres at rear of car modified; body lengthened to 15ft 3¾in; optional axle ratios 3.45:1 (manual) and 3.07:1 (automatic) offered; engine insulation upgraded; front seats revised; passenger door locking now remote; switch gear revised; fuse box moved to glove box; larger ashtray fitted; fuel tank shape modified.

PRICE NEW: £9,500

Series 4
'Oscar India'
October 1978 – January 1986
Changes were evolutionary throughout the fourth series. From chassis number:

V812032 - Rear boot spoiler fitted; dashboard redesigned with wood trim; leather head lining fitted; air-conditioning upgraded; shock absorbers revised; cruise control offered on automatic cars; gas struts fitted to bonnet. Engine improvements included revised pistons and cam profiles; tuftrided valves; and increased compression ratio.

PRICE NEW: £23,000

Series 5
January 1986–October 1989
From chassis number:

V812500 - Weber-Marelli fuel injection replaced carburettors; bonnet bulge flattened. BBS alloy wheels fitted.

PRICE NEW: £55,000

PRODUCTION FIGURES:

Series 2	289
Chassis numbers: V8/10501 to V8/10789	
Series 3	921
Chassis numbers: V8/11102 to V8/12000 and V8/12010 to V812031	
Series 4	468
Chassis numbers: V8/12032 to V8/12499	
Series 5	202
Chassis numbers: V8/12500 to V8/12701	

that has been 'updated', and not always happily. The updated engine in the original bodywork would, on the face of it, be the best of all possible worlds, but in fact the bulk of the later engines really only gained smoothness as opposed to poke. It would seem from the foregoing that the first Bosch-injected engines were as powerful as the last Weber/Marelli ones. But, there was more.

Aston Martin *Nimrod*

If the 'cooking' versions of this long-lived V8 were standing still, elsewhere there were some changes. A peek at what was going on was offered to AMOC members at the St John Horsfall memorial meeting at Silverstone in June 1976, when a car appeared, driven by Mike Loasby, Aston Martin's director of engineering. It was only a demonstration run, but clearly there was something rather different about the car.

Basically, it was producing the thick end of 400bhp. Revisions to valves, camshafts, manifolding and carburation had between them released 60bhp over the contemporary 'series 3' saloon, to produce the ultimate 'bruiser', capable of 170mph (274kph) with acceleration to match. Heads turned. Obviously Marek's engine was waking up at last. What was most remarkable, though, was that these improvements, which liberated so much extra grunt, were to evolve relatively quickly and, more vitally, with reliability.

Of course, privateers had been breathing on the V8 for some time. Midlands Aston Martin specialist Robin Hamilton had entered the lists in 1974 with the first of a series of modifications that were to lead to his entry in the 1977 Le Mans 24-hour race. In fact, while Loasby was haring around Silverstone, Hamilton was just coming to terms with the lack of funding for him to enter the 1976 race, for he at least felt that he and the car were both ready.

Hamilton undertook a vast programme of modification to his car, which had started out as a DBSV8, chassis number 10038; so much so that by the time he found some sponsorship he had re-numbered the chassis as RHAM001. The engine output, with 50mm Weber carburettors, altered valves and Cosworth pistons, was producing in excess of 500bhp and 400lb ft of torque, which made Loasby's Silverstone mount look a mite wimpish.

But RHAM001 was a pure racer, fibreglass and tank tape being much in evidence, whereas the factory car as demonstrated by Loasby was civilised, and, of course, was to form the basis of a production car. Hamilton pressed on, and in conjunction with David Preece and Mike Salmon succeeded in achieving a creditable 17th place in the 1977 Le Mans race.

The 1978 event was financially beyond Hamilton, but in 1979 he returned, this time with forced induction in the form of twin Garrett turbochargers; this gave a whopping 800bhp at 6,000rpm, which was possibly a little hysterical. Clearly, however, the basic architecture of the engine was capable of huge development. But this was not the end of Hamilton, despite RHAM001's modest achievements; he would re-enter the story quite soon.

After the factory had proved to their own satisfaction that the engine output could be tweaked so much, there was a rush of private efforts to accomplish the same thing. Some of the results were outrageous, with almost 100bhp per litre routinely produced, and with quite good reliability. Many of the Aston Martin specialists had their own particular methodology, the costs of which were huge; more than one retail customer drew the line at paying such high service bills to subsidise racing. As a result, more and more specialists appeared who were able to concentrate on just servicing cars. In the middle 1980s many a comparative discussion on the relative merits of this or that specialist would be defined by 'do they race?'

By the end of 1981 it was clear that the privateers (and the factory) had more than enough expertise to develop the Marek V8 for serious competition use, but the prospect of a front-engined car being remotely competitive was a distant one. Hamilton, of course, already knew this and had contacted Eric Broadley, the patron of Lola, and Britain's premier GT manufacturer, to build a tub and shell as a commercial proposition. Broadley had already produced the famous Lola T70 series, about which Aston Martin were more familiar than they probably cared to be, as well as being the design brains behind the Ford GT40 project. The new car would be called Nimrod.

The catalyst for the effective re-entry of the Aston Martin marque into racing was that Pace petroleum had bought into the company. The boss of Pace

was Victor Gauntlett – businessman, oil trader and, almost inevitably, committed car buff. Born in 1942, Gauntlett had founded Pace petroleum at the age of 30, after working for BP and Total.

By late 1981 Hamilton had parlayed this arrangement with Broadley into Nimrod Racing Automobiles, a financially uneven tripartite arrangement between himself, Gauntlett and Peter Livanos, scion of the Greek shipping dynasty. For Livanos it was fun, for Hamilton it was a great relief, and for Gauntlett it was a chance to create a momentum for his newly acquired investment. As things transpired, Nemesis would have been a more appropriate appellation.

Gauntlett's view, sensibly, was that the engines would be works items,

developed by Aston Martin Tickford, as the tuning arm was now called. This was perfectly fine, but the dead hand of FIA regulation immediately twitched and, overnight, made the Nimrod project obsolete. New rules calmly sliced off 200kg (441lb) from the minimum weight requirements and allowed ground effects. Immediately lighter, more advanced cars were in the lists and the Nimrod was an instant anachronism. Livanos could see that the whole project was more or less scuppered and withdrew. Gauntlett, committed to the venture on more than one level, could not. He also viewed the development budget of the Tickford engines as an investment in the road cars. In this he was quite right, but he was to discover quite soon what David Brown as well as a generation of others, from Herbert Austin to Louis Zborowski, had: that

Three generations of Aston Martin racer: Ulster (left) and DB3S front the 1980s Nimrod.

the cost of effectively scratch-building engines and ancillaries to racing tolerances was certainly not a task for the faint-hearted.

Whatever the achievements of the Nimrod project, and they were, in competition terms, very few, there were several benefits for the consolidation of the development work on engines, which was, of course, why Gauntlett had sanctioned participation in the first place. The results, in terms of the progress towards producing ever more powerful road cars, were clear. The Vantage engine tune, as a result, developed apace.

V8 Vantage
and Volante

The V8 Vantage actually predated Nimrod. The early works effort to uprate the V8, as exemplified by Loasby's demonstration run at Silverstone, was to lead to a production model relatively quickly. It was ready by February 1977 and, not surprisingly, was quickly established as the fastest-accelerating production car in the world.

Chronologically, the Vantage appeared when the 'series 3' V8 was in production, and the visual differences were fairly obvious. A separate boot spoiler and blanked-off radiator grille and bonnet intake were the most noticeable, but the new deep chin spoiler was a novelty, and not to everyone's liking.

When the 'series 4' Oscar India arrived, the Vantage cars were updated in keeping with it, so the rather hastily applied boot spoiler was modified to be more in keeping. Mechanically, the car was more or less unchanged, but the series 3 had already benefited from the development of the Vantage, in that special tuning options had become available, so customers could have the Vantage state of tune applied to their series 3 cars. That not many opted to do so makes the hotter series 3 cars very scarce.

As the series 3 gave way to the series 4, another variant, the Volante, appeared. The long-awaited convertible had been the subject of much clamouring in North America since the middle of the 1970s, but due to the unavoidable problems of reorganisation and the tightness of funds, the project was not undertaken until the fortunes of Aston Martin Lagonda (1975) were secured. Budgets had to be set aside for the development of the new Lagonda, so work did not begin on the car until 1977. It was, pleasingly, carried out under the supervision of Harold Beach who, it must be said, knew this chassis better than anyone, having basically designed it over 20 years before.

One of the reasons why it was possible to consider the Volante for production was the fact that Jensen Motors, which had gone the same way as Company Developments, had failed to find itself a buyer, so its Interceptor convertible was no more, leaving a large gap in the market. Beach set to work to fill it. It was his last project for the firm; in the spring of 1978 he finally retired.

Some of the features found on the Oscar India car were anticipated in the Volante, which first appeared in June 1978, while the series 3 was being built. Among them were the distinctive blanked-off bonnet scoop and the wooden trim in the cabin. All the initial run of Volantes were destined for the North American market, for while the company had been having problems at home, the plight of the American operation had been dire. Although they had never actually closed their doors, they had been very close to doing so, being forced to survive on repairs, servicing and parts. The inability to meet emission regulations through the early 1970s had hit sales hard, and they sorely needed something new to sell. As soon as the model was announced, AML North America boldly booked a year's production.

With the Oscar India the range became normalised into saloon, Vantage and Volante. There was great

With a host of aerodynamic excrescenses the series 3 now looked frankly tarty

reluctance to offer a Vantage Volante, the main reason being that it was going to be very difficult to persuade the hood to stay on at high speed, and in open form the aerodynamics of the car might produce odd handling. There was, after all, no hardtop available.

So the Volante remained more or less unchanged through the production of the series 4 saloon; the car did not adopt the tail spoiler of the Oscar India or Vantage until it was updated, which coincided with the series 5 V8; at this point the AMOC refers to the Volante as a series 2, despite the fact that it featured the Weber/Marelli fuel injection and the flat bonnet line of the series 5.

There was also a series 3 Volante, if one is going to nit-pick, which was the long-awaited Vantage version, available from November 1986. By its side skirts shall ye know it. It was this model that really hammered home the point that the core design was becoming tired by now, with a host of

aerodynamic excrescences from the boot spoiler to the extended wheel arches. They were all quite necessary to put up with the vast power output of the engine, but to many observers the car looked frankly tarty.

Aston Martin agreed. It was no longer enough that the cars were at the peak of their technical development; the better-funded competition were producing machines that were not only as fast, but were also much more 'all of a piece'. Simply re-bodying the car was not a long-term option, but there was one route, which had not been taken for a quarter century, which seemed worth trying.

From a driving point of view it is hard not to be a vulgarian about the AM Vantage. It is so fast for its type that parallels are elusive. It disappoints only in one particular, which is that so little of the grunt is really usable. The throttle response is very fast and sets the car twisting on its springs when standing still; when under way the torque of the engine will launch the car into the middle distance in more or less any gear, but if one follows the normal sequence, the temptation simply to carry on going to the aerodynamic limit is disquieting.

Under braking the weight transference is rather obvious, and on a wet road the car could, I imagine, be something of a handful. Around corners it behaves impeccably – until it doesn't. In a straight line it simply does not back off at all. I was unable to detect any kink in the power curve whatever, and the sense of acceleration stays with you until at least 140mph (225kph), after which it tails off – a bit. If I still had reservations about the DBSV8, the Vantage did nothing to dispel them. I think that you have to be a very good driver indeed to get the best out of it, for it is not quite as forgiving as its predecessors and probably very easy to drive badly. You also need to like big cars; for someone weaned on a

Aston Martin V8, Volante and Vantage production

Figures courtesy of the Aston Martin Owners' Club.
Between April 1972 and October 1989 a bewildering variety of cars were made (mainly) to a common theme:

NUMBERS BUILT:

V8 saloon Series 2	288
Series 3	967
Series 4	352
Series 5	405
V8 Volante Series 1	656
V8 Volante Series 2	245
V8 Vantage Series 1	38, plus 13 Vantage look-alikes for the US market
V8 Vantage Series 2	304, plus 14 Vantage look-alikes for the US market
V8 Vantage Volante	166
V8 Vantage Volante 'PoW spec'	26, plus 56 Vantage Volante look-alikes for the US market
V8 Vantage Zagato	52
V8 Vantage Volante Zagato	37
Total:	3,619
Plus DBSV8s (402)	4,021

Common dimensions including wheelbase and track as for the DBSV8.

little Alfa, for example, I should imagine that it would be a daunting prospect, at least initially.

But inevitably it shrinks as you settle into it and you realise that all is well. This is not as crazy a car as the rumours would have you believe because there is rather more to it than merely a more powerful engine. Although the brakes have only cursory modification (the discs are grooved), the suspension is harder and this is comforting: the thought of any inexactitude over ripply surfaces with an engine of this power output under the bonnet is disturbing. Even so, the stiffer springs, coupled with this mighty engine, can make for some interesting moments. Be in no doubt that this car needs careful handling and the cost of some advanced driving lessons should be added to the price if you are considering buying one.

The Volante.

Aston Martin
V8 Zagato

Prototypes and speculative specials aside, it had been 25 years since Aston Martin had produced a two-seater; the DB4GT had, as a homologated special, been a sales success and the firm saw a chance to repeat the idea of a short-run, short-chassis road car based on the existing model. In the case of the DB4GT Zagato, it had been a very short run indeed, with no two cars exactly the same; the planned new model was to be a little more standardised than that, although it was to be the work of the same coachbuilder.

The market for exotic cars was boiling merrily at the time that the model was mooted, with waiting lists building even for the 'cooking' models offered by Newport Pagnell. Porsche had introduced the 959 and Ferrari the 288 GTO, both of which were extremely complex, advanced and consequently costly. There were queues of buyers, many of whom were speculators whose plan was merely to sit on the cars, undriven, until the market would offer them a fair return. For a while it worked well enough for Newport Pagnell to jump on the bandwagon.

The V8 Zagato was, however, never conceived as a complex supercar; it lacked even anti-lock brakes, for example. Its spiritual progenitor, the DB4GT, had been a shortened and tweaked DB4 saloon, and the same recipe was intended here: lighten and shorten the chassis, drop in an engine in the highest state of tune, and leave it to the driver to sort out how it works.

There was a broad specification that Aston Martin calculated would be needed: a top speed in the order of 300kph (186mph) and acceleration from 0–60mph (97kph) in around 5 seconds. In order to accomplish this, it was calculated that the engine would need to produce around 400bhp in a body with a drag coefficient (Cd) of 0.29 and a final drive of 3.06:1.

None of these requirements was a particular problem, save the axle ratio, but a new crown wheel and pinion set was easily sourced from Salisbury. The highest current state of tune of the AM V8 in road-going form was around 380bhp, although the racing versions of the engine had produced 100bhp per litre as far back as 1983, so a reliable 12 per cent increase in bhp was not a particular obstacle. The Cd figure was up to Zagato.

A commensurate reduction in weight was obviously desirable. Sixteen inches (406mm) was taken from the V8 chassis, virtually eliminating the rear overhang of Beach's design. The first modified platform was shipped out to Zagato in Milan in February 1985 and a static model was prepared in time for the Frankfurt

The V8 Zagato.

The frontal treatment, with its unsightly bonnet bulge, is not to everyone's taste.

Motor Show in September. The initial plan was to build 50 cars, and the response was such that deposits were received for enough of them that the exercise was into paper profit immediately.

The car resembled, but did not adhere strictly to, the initial styling sketches. It had been planned that the 400bhp needed to propel this extraordinary car would come from the application of Weber/Marelli fuel injection to the current Vantage engine, which would allow a flat bonnet line; in the event, the modification to the fuel injection system was beyond the budget available, so carburettors were used. They were massive 50mm Weber down-draught units and, unsurprisingly, sat high above the engine, necessitating a bonnet bulge that many, quite rightly, thought unsightly. It was really a re-run of the early V8 evolution.

The Cd figure finally came out at 0.33, which was creditable but caused no one to swoon. If 300kph was to be achieved, and, more important the acceleration to go with it, even more grunt was needed. It transpired that enough experience had been gained from the special tuning of customer cars for the V8 to deliver it with relative ease. According to Michael Bowler, then Technical Director:

'We had developed a Vantage for a South African owner with enlarged carburettor chokes, new cams, higher compression and big-bore exhaust, which developed 430–440bhp. By fitting this engine to a stripped-out development Vantage – with 150kg removed to give the Zagato's weight and distribution – 60mph was reached in under 5 seconds.'

With the addition of lightweight seats and various other weight-saving schemes, most of which ensured that the car remained somewhat under-equipped, the final specification was reasonably close to the original concept. All that remained to be done was to actually run the car at 300kph.

Roy Salvadori, the man who had given Aston Martin their 1959 Le Mans victory, was drafted in as test driver, which was a nice touch. After some niggling trouble, he was clocked at 299kph, just short of 186mph, but, it was felt, 'close enough'. Salvadori had been the man who had first broken the 300kph barrier at Le Mans in another Zagato-inspired missile, the Project 214 race car.

The V8 Zagato was a simple statement of the marque's identity: well-built, robust, very fast and possessed of sufficient handling finesse to please anyone. Above all, it was essentially relatively simple. To an emerging market of technophiles, weaned on turbochargers, ABS and traction control, it appeared almost agricultural, and to some of them, who have not enjoyed its charms, it remains so.

But the most spectacular point about the V8 Zagato was what happened to its price. As the speculative end of the classic car movement acquired its own momentum, it was relatively simple for AML Ltd to buy back buyers' deposits at a profit and solicit new deposits from the apparently endless line of property developers, money brokers and investment bankers who were queuing up to buy. Thus, the list price of the new car effortlessly rose; apparently (and this is, of course, a thing to which few people would admit now) the practice was widespread across Europe, leading to one luckless punter paying £1,000,000 for a 'pre-owned' Ferrari F40 when the list price was something in the region of £110,000. When the music stopped, of course, it

The AMR racers

Hope springs eternal, and Victor Gauntlett grabbed with both hands the first chance to re-enter the world of formal competition. His view that the AML engines were strong enough and reliable enough to 'make the cut' in racing terms had to an extent been borne out by the Nimrod project, costly and lowering though it had been.

This time round, however, Gauntlett and Peter Livanos were determined to build their own chassis and enter the car as an Aston Martin rather than an Aston-engined special. Work commenced under the supervision of Max Boxtrom, late of Brabham, in early 1987. It was to be a six-year project and, after Ford had politely rejected an Aston Martin funded return to racing, Livanos happily agreed to bear the entire cost.

Where the Nimrod had been a slightly speculative special, the AMR was not. The role of John Wyer, as racing manager, fell to Richard Williams, who had managed Viscount Downe's Nimrod as well as the re-invented Ecurie Ecosse group C2 project. Design had moved on since the days of the Nimrod and the AMR racers were to enjoy more or less every refinement. Williams had also learned much.

The car was constructed along F1 lines, with a central structure of carbon fibre and kevlar, so despite its superficial resemblance to the mighty Le Mans cars of the 1970s, it was as modern in its design as Boxtrom could make it, with a clever venturi-effect tail and a separate spoiler. The engine was a 6-litre version of the four-valve unit under development by Reeves Callaway for the Virage project.

The car had a promising debut at Dijon in 1989 and ran well again at Le Mans, where it carried a black stripe as a mark of respect to John Wyer, who had died that April. Overall, the showing of the AMR racer was very promising, but motor sport regulation moves along almost as fast as the cars. Capacity limits fell, and although the prospect of the 3½-litre Ford V8 becoming available for years ahead was a mouth-watering one, sadly it was not to be; Jaguar were to get it.

The Zagato V8 has its own style of dashboard. Is there a hint of the old Aston instrument binnacle to be seen?

all got rather nasty. Someone (it may even have been the same 'investor') was rumoured to have taken a loss of over £600,000 on one Ferrari. This was when our friend the cheery psychopath received some well-merited therapy.

This was an environment in which neither the V8 Zagato nor its manufacturer could expect to prosper in the long term. As values flattened off, then started to plunge, a generation of losers was established, many of whom would never again (they said) make the same mistake. But for Aston Martin as a company it had been a profitable exercise, and as was well known Newport Pagnell had enjoyed precious few of those.

Driving impressions of the V8 Zagato are quite startling; it is without doubt the quickest car I have ever driven and, all in all, quite memorable. I had no chance to explore very much beyond the legal limit, so my

impressions are limited to the twisty Sussex roads where I exercised it. Anyway, like all Aston V8s the lower gears are where the fun is, and tyre-shredding standing starts are not really a feature of sensible driving. However, road testers reporting 0–60mph (97kph) in 4.8 seconds cannot be exaggerating much. Overall, apart from a discernibly smaller cabin, the sensation is like driving any other V8, but on fast forward – very easy, I think, to get completely carried away. Overall, with the same wheelbase and track as a V8 saloon, the handling characteristics are not radically different, but the smaller body and uncompromising mechanicals make this as involving a car to drive as its spiritual progenitor, the DB4GT.

The lack of ABS is hardly a problem at sensible speeds. However, I should imagine that one would rather miss it when trying to scrub off 150mph on a damp German autobahn, with the usual 38-car Teutonic lemmings' pile-up visible in the near distance. Mind you, if you do find yourself in that situation, you probably deserve to become number 39.

Jaw-dropping though the performance of this car is, I am not sure that it is for me. I am pleased that it was made, as the mere fact that such machines exist is, I think, rather splendid, but there are some irritating little inconsistencies that betray a lack of thought. Possibly the

The market was never really the squirearchy - that was just PR

most absurd is that the handbook will not fit into the glove box, but that is mere scribbler nit-picking. Worse is the window arrangement, with smaller opening panels in the main glass. Due to the curvature and shape of the Maserati-sourced doors (similar to the ones found on the Biturbo), there is no other arrangement that will work. It's rather a kit-car touch, but probably better than side-screens.

After the V8 Vantage, the Zagato was a revelation to me. Where the

Vantage felt ludicrously overpowered, or underdeveloped, the Zagato felt much more of a piece. Any car powered by a version of the highly tuned Marek V8 is a challenge to drive well and with discipline, and the Zagato, with its uncompromising objectives, goes further than its peers towards allowing the driver to achieve that. There are no surprises with the Zagato – it looks the part, is the part and delivers the goods, and that alone is worthy of some celebration.

Is it possible to drive and enjoy these hugely fast cars and still feel comfortable in a DB4? I think so. No matter how many owners Aston Martin has had, there are certain imperatives in the design and construction of these cars that simply bellow at you as you become involved with them. Consider this: the Harold

Beach chassis has carried these cars, in one form or another, for over 40 years since the DB4. To be sure, it has been modified and improved, had a de Dion added to it, the suspension and drive characteristics have been altered, and the power increased by almost 100 per cent, but there is an expectation of what you will get when you climb into one of these and, in that sense, they are all of a piece. It is pleasing. Knowledge of the six-cylinder cars can, however, hold you back as you drive the V8s – you almost run out of expectations, until you remember the engine and what it will deliver. A 7-litre Zagato, of which there are few around, has a torque curve like an iron bar. I did not manage to drive one, unfortunately. Nor did I sample the even rarer Volante, which first saw the light of day in March 1987.

By now, the image of the marque was no longer really that of rat-catcher trousers and hairy tweed hacking-jackets (the marketplace for the cars had never really been the squirearchy anyway; that was merely a public relations angle). While the cars had once photographed well in stable yards and in front of coaching inns, Aston Martin was now in a very competitive marketplace indeed, and had come a long way from Mr Goldstone's days. Opposition in the 'supercar' market was now coming at them from all sides and there was some concern that Newport Pagnell was standing still. No, it wasn't.

The bonnet bulge is necessitated by the intake manifolding.

Aston Martin *Virage*

The Virage, when it was announced, drew praise for its timeless styling. Testers, however, were not as impressed when they drove it.

In a sense the Virage was ten years late. Alan Curtis remembered thinking that the V8 was outdated by 1976, and arguably only the phenomenal increases in power that had been liberated from it, giving it a new lease of life, had kept it in production. From any perspective, it was showing its age a little by 1986. In Volante Vantage form, spoilered, skirted and looking thoroughly uncomfortable, the car's basic shape was clearly 19 years old. Only the fact that it was such a remarkable machine that oozed technical competence allowed the series of questionable facelifts to continue. To uncritical serial buyers of the V8 range, part of the fun was to carry out their own modifications anyway, or, more commonly, to get someone else to do so.

Clearly, the V8 would not survive another dubious makeover – a new model was required, and by the 1988 Motor Show it was ready. The exercise was something more than the re-bodying of the old car. No one expected a firm like Aston Martin Lagonda to take a great leap in the dark and produce a totally new model, but the V8 had lost much ground as a benchmark since its introduction.

So, within months of the introduction of the final version of the V8, discussions took place as to what its replacement should look like. In keeping with the tradition that had survived through so many changes, the undertaking was designated Development Project 2034. The broad specification followed that of the V8: front engine, rear-wheel drive, very fast, and comfortable. A further critical point was that the engine needed to meet the global regulations for the use of lead-free fuel that were clearly on the way. The decision was made to use Reeves Callaway Engineering in Connecticut, USA, as consultants to the project, which was

Clearly the V8 would not survive another makeover - a new model was required

to give the Marek V8 its first structural makeover for 20 years. Callaway's expertise in the development of four-valve V8 cylinder heads for both racing and road cars was considered to be vital to the 'cleaning up' of the V8 to allow it to work with catalytic converters for the first time and, later, other ancillaries.

Callaway commenced work in the spring of 1986. Their brief was to develop a catalysed four-valve engine with a power output equivalent to the existing 305bhp of the 'series 5' V8, so that even with power-sapping emission controls the car would perform as well as or better than the current model. Allowance was to be made for a more powerful version, which would, in all probability employ forced induction to raise its game when the time came, which it surely would.

Aston Martin Virage
October 1988–October 1996

ENGINE:
V8, alloy block and heads

Bore x stroke	85 x 100mm
Capacity	5340cc
Valves	Twin ohc per bank, four valves per cylinder
Compression ratio	9.5:1
Fuel system	Weber fuel injection
Power	310bhp at 6,000rpm

TRANSMISSION:
ZF five-speed manual, or Chrysler Torqueflite automatic. Four-speed automatic gearbox from 1993

SUSPENSION:
Front: Unequal length wishbones, coil springs, co-axial spring dampers, anti-roll bar
Back: Alloy de Dion axle, triangulated radius arms, Watt linkage, coil springs, telescopic dampers
Steering: Adwest power-assisted rack and pinion

BRAKES:
Lockheed ventilated discs, outboard front and rear

WHEELS:
Aston Martin alloy, 8 x 16-inch

BODYWORK:
Four-seater, two-door alloy body, designed by Heffernan and Greenley. Hand-built, fitted with flush glass, deformable bumpers and boot-lid spoiler. Drophead Volante offered from October 1990. Chassis: Steel platform type, extensively modified from, but similar to, previous V8 model

LENGTH:	15ft 6½in (4.74m)
WIDTH:	6ft 1in (1.85m)
WHEELBASE:	8ft 6¾in (2.61m)
HEIGHT:	4ft 4in (1.32m)
WEIGHT:	35.7cwt (1,816kg)
MAX SPEED:	155mph (249kph)
PRICE NEW:	£120,000

In side profile, the proportions are distinctly DB4-like.

The development of the chassis and body was to be carried out in the UK; the former was to be modified at Newport Pagnell, while the body design was put out to tender. One problem encountered fairly quickly was that if the new car was to be able to outbrake itself, the discs would take much punishment. The racing versions of the V8, as developed by customers, had shown that an undue build-up of heat on the inboard rear brakes could cause problems with the oil seals on the cheeks of the differential. This had only been overcome by the fitting of oil coolers for the differential unit, which was, to say the least, a nuisance, and on a road car merely something else to worry about. The inboard brakes were also a nuisance when it came to changing pads. It was therefore decided to move the rear brakes outboard; this would increase unsprung weight, but that was a price

worth paying. The V8 had a deserved reputation for heavy differential wear, and it might also help to obviate that.

As to where the brakes would come from, the answer was Australia; it appeared that no European manufacturer had the capacity to make them. Whereas the old inboard mounted discs had been of a manageable size, the specification now called for 13-inch vented discs at the front and 11.3-inch at the rear.

The body design was awarded to John Heffernan and Ken Greenley, who were both tutors at the Royal College of Art. They enlisted the help of Southampton University's wind tunnel to produce a shape that pleased both the traditionalists and those looking for something more innovative. It was the classic coupé profile and all agreed that it was much prettier than the series 5 V8. The Cd figure was

0.35, which was a small disappointment, being the same as for the DB4, but the rear end was, aerodynamically at least, well tied down.

However, no one will be surprised to learn that underneath the svelte new body sat a chassis that, by way of the 1970s Lagonda saloon, owed much to the previous work of Harold Beach. When William Towns had designed the Lagonda, he had stretched Beach's design; now the Virage was to shrink it back again as well as incorporating some new rear-end features. Not surprisingly, the resulting chassis proportions were, in all cases, within a millimetre of Beach's original core design. It had apparently been hoped originally to design a brand new chassis for the Virage, but time, cost

and the full knowledge that the existing one worked perfectly well made it avoidable. It was the outside of the existing car that was dated, not its underpinnings.

The 'mule' for the Virage was a two-door version of the Lagonda (actually quite an elegant thing in itself), which happily ran around from early 1988 with Callaway's engine installed.

Looking at the Virage, one is unavoidably reminded of the DB4 series of cars; it is not so much an exercise in retro-styling, more a reaffirmation of the proportions of the earlier models, which have always been pleasing. The high waistline, the proportion of the bonnet length to the wheelbase, the caricature grille, all are trademarks of the original

The rear three-quarter view. The basic shape remains today, although the cars no longer bear the Virage name.

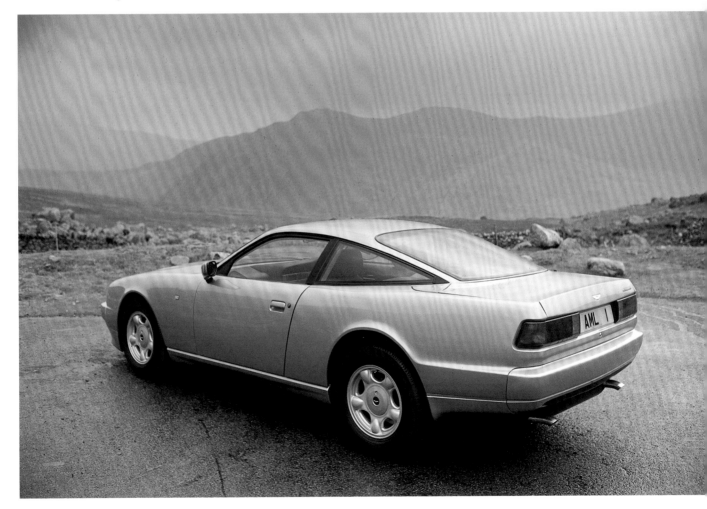

The Virage line at Newport Pagnell. Ford took the view that there was rather too much of it.

Touring design, but are nicely blended into a shape that is undeniably an Aston Martin, but clearly not an old one.

The car would be manufactured in the same way as its predecessors, the body being built up with hand-rolled and welded alloy panels over cut steel formers that were pre-attached to the chassis. It was as time-consuming as ever, but all agreed that the results were worth it. If the car looked bland, it was merely so in contrast to the stubbily extravagant Zagato and the mutton-dressed-as-lamb bespoilered V8. Its shape represented a natural evolution, born of the sense of continuity that the designers felt was part and parcel of their job.

The over-engineering that had characterised the original DB4 chassis, 30 years before, remained.

The car was still heavy, fast and expensive, of course, for it was an Aston, but under the bonnet great changes had been wrought. The price was an all-up weight of 35.7cwt (1,816kg), but then it was trimmed to a level of luxury that marked a departure for the firm (and which made up much of the weight difference) and set a new standard for the opposition.

The reception given to the Virage was enthusiastic, but stopped just short of wild. One journal summed it up as a 'classy Calibra', which was certainly not the effect sought. The performance was, by anyone's standards, huge, but the handling was initially no better than the old V8 model and, under some circumstances, even wayward. There was some hint of imprecision in the architecture of the rear end, for example, so that at the colossal speeds of which the car was capable the driver would have to correct the steering rather too much. There was, in fact, a hint of rear-end steering, not unlike that from which the early E-Type Jaguar suffered, and certainly not part of the original design specification.

The answer lay in the triangulated rear chassis sub-frame that carried the de Dion, clearly inspired by that best-handling of marques, Alfa Romeo. Its mounting was insufficiently rigid, and as a result the car could wander. One of the development engineers was unwise enough to comment that the new structure cost as much as a Ford Sierra to manufacture, which was tactless of him, given that Ford had taken control of the company part way through the Virage project, and that when all was said and done it did not actually work properly. He left

the firm, the design was soon rectified, and work could go ahead on developing the Virage in drophead (Volante) and Vantage form to produce a cluster of machines that today are known at the factory simply as 'V' cars.

The Virage may well be a supremely elegant car, but when I came to drive one I have to say that it left me totally unmoved. The first manifestation of the Callaway-tuned engine is certainly a revelation of efficiency, but overall the Virage is a great leap sideways. The initial road testers were right: the rear end of the car is vague and lacks feel; the rear axle location is far superior on the V8; and, unsurprisingly, it was to this set-up, or a version of it, that the factory would revert when that chariot of the Gods, the Vantage, appeared. I must confess that I am prepared to be persuaded that I was

Yet again, new levels of comfort were introduced with the Virage.

prejudiced going into this by unnerving tales of 'wander', but, tyro that I am in terms of road testing, I think I knew what they meant.

But despite that I do rather like the look of it. The proportions are pleasingly bottom heavy, aircraft-carrier like, and while one might initially assume that the car is rather claustrophobic inside, it is not the

Was this not an Aston Martin one might suspect that the comforts were a distraction from something unpleasant

case at all. However, one is quite unused to this level of trim. Were this not an Aston Martin, I might have thought that all this comfort was drawing my attention away from something unpleasant. I am used to plainer stuff.

The delights of the de Dion axle on the earlier cars are plainly compromised on the Virage and it does not encourage you to drive it hard. Aurally it is weaker than its predecessor, and the introduction of the performance-enhancing 6.3-litre conversion in 1991, complete with suspension modifications (they did catch that quite early on), really rather says it all. It is, if anything, sedate and thus something of a let-down. However, to be fair to it, it was transformed before long into a completely marvellous machine.

The four-valve Callaway-developed engine. Catalysed, it would work anywhere.

The Virage, sadly, was the last of these cars that I drove for the purposes of this book; more thorough descriptions of the new models are available from the pens of those who are much more experienced than me, so I do not presume to pass comment upon them. I have had a quick burst in a Vantage, and that was quite enough to persuade me that they have got it right now.

Harold Beach's chassis design was finally retired with the Virage. As a rule, the V8 coupé, Volante and Vantage are now made to special order only, for a new product was in the pipeline, one that had been dear to Victor Gauntlett's heart for some time.

Aston Martin DB7

Any time a journalist cared to ask him, and they often did, Victor Gauntlett was keen to point out that the target set by Aston Martin was to produce a volume car as close as possible to the spirit of the DB4. While this meant that it would be no bargain (the DB4, hardly a volume car, cost as much as two XK150 coupés, and still does), Gauntlett was of the opinion that

Aston Martin would be going for Porsche's market, albeit in a smaller way. The cherished undertaking was named DP1999, but not, I think, as a result of any numerical sequence; it merely had a millennial feel to it.

You can build cars sentimentally, or you can build them commercially. David Brown had been somewhere in the middle; as an industrialist (and a

The DB7 with its DB4 Vantage ancestor.

Yorkshireman) he was just about able to rationalise the simply vast expense of running Aston Martin, together with racing, as a proper adjunct to his core business. Company Developments were opportunists driven by perceived asset values. Gauntlett, whose commercial interests lay in the oil market, and who therefore clearly knew how many beans made five, was not by training a manufacturer, with all that that implies; he therefore had trouble carrying through his ambition on a commercial level, although enthusiasts quite saw his point (but they, of course, were not having to underwrite it). He was, in short, a bit stuck.

The first hint of what was to come took place at the Mille Miglia retrospective in the spring of 1987. Gauntlett, co-driving a DBR sports racer with Prince Michael of Kent, met Walter and Elizabeth Hayes at the villa of Gordon and Joyce Wilkins,

Hayes knew that large companies can often learn from small ones

near Brescia. It was an agreeable house party. Over dinner Gauntlett confided to Hayes that he had ambitions to develop a higher-volume, more accessible car than the V8, but frankly lacked the capital to bring his idea to fruition. His pride in the heritage of Aston Martin was clear, and was neatly punctuated by the flamboyant arrival of Prince Michael in a DBR2 with an adoring Italian police escort. The conversation passed on to other things and, all too soon, the nostalgic interlude was over.

Back in the UK, Hayes dropped in on his close friend, Henry Ford II, who kept a house near Henley. As Hayes recollected to me, Ford said 'Well, Walter, what are we going to do today?' Hayes responded 'Well, we

Aston Martin DB7
February 1994

ENGINE:
Straight six-cylinder, alloy block and heads

Capacity	3226cc
Valves	Twin ohc, four valves per cylinder
Compression ratio	8.3:1
Fuel system	Zytec multi-point fuel injection, Eaton belt-driven supercharger
Power	335bhp at 5,600rpm

TRANSMISSION:
Getrag five-speed manual, or GM four-speed automatic

SUSPENSION:
Front: Independent double wishbone, anti-dive geometry. Coil springs and telescopic dampers
Back: Independent double wishbone, longitudinal control arms and coil springs
Steering: Power-assisted rack and pinion

BRAKES:
Lockheed ventilated discs, outboard front and rear

WHEELS:
Aston Martin alloy, 8 x 18-inch

BODYWORK:
Four-seater, two-door mainly steel body with some composite panels, designed by Ian Callum. Hand-built, fitted with flush glass, deformable bumpers. Lift-out roof panel. Convertible Volante model offered from October 1996. Chassis: Steel platform type, extensively modified from, but similar to, Jaguar XJS floorpan

LENGTH:	15ft 2in (4.62m)
WIDTH:	5ft 11¾in (1.82m)
WHEELBASE:	8ft 6in (2.59m)
HEIGHT:	4ft 2½in (1.28m)
WEIGHT:	33.9cwt (1,723kg)
MAX SPEED:	165mph (265kph)
PRICE NEW:	£78,000

could always buy Aston Martin.'

This was not merely light conversation. Hayes knew, through his association with Colin Chapman, Eric Broadley and Keith Duckworth, not to mention John Wyer, that large companies can frequently learn from small ones, or more correctly that they can re-learn things that they have perforce forgotten. After all, with a tiny budget Hayes had provided the raison d'être for Cosworth Engineering more than 20 years before. Before that, his role in the development of the GT40 road racing car, when he had worked closely with John Wyer, had taught him that the values of a small operation are precious indeed, and,

once lost, are seldom if ever recovered. He further pointed out, as if Henry didn't know it, that Ford had not made a major acquisition since they bought Lincoln back in 1931. Of course, he also knew that Ford had their eye on a major European manufacturer, probably Jaguar, and probably soon.

Henry Ford II was a close friend of both David Brown and George Livanos, Peter's uncle. It was not difficult to work out what was needed for Aston Martin. All were impressed at the way in which Gauntlett had husbanded the skills resources of the

Now began the job of unifying what it was that AML represented

firm, and, the horrendous racing expenses aside, how he had run it in a thoroughly businesslike but properly small-scale manner.

Events took on a momentum of their own, and quite swiftly. By July 1987, at a dinner at Ford UK's London headquarters in Gower Street, the basics of a deal were defined. Ford would buy 75 per cent of the equity of Aston Martin, and Gauntlett would stay on for a period of three years as Chief Executive, his other interests permitting. Ford would have no financial involvement in any Aston Martin racing activities, and nor would Aston Martin; that was non-negotiable. Any racing activity would have to be funded by other sources. Walter Hayes, the architect of this, would maintain a watching brief.

Hayes was careful. Such an insubstantial thing as company

The rear three-quarter view of the DB7.

morale, not to mention brand identity, that elusive quality that can be described as where the public sees the image of the product, is easily smashed by benign neglect, and is hard to rebuild. The process of consolidating what it was that Aston Martin represented then began. Tragically, however, as the press releases confirming the acquisition were being prepared, Henry Ford II died, and was not to see the project through to fruition. Ford's death shook Hayes, but also energised him.

Soon after buying Aston Martin, Ford also bought Jaguar, after a very expensive bidding war that had brought beads of sweat to many a forehead at Dearborn, Ford's global HQ. The bringing together, potentially, of the two famous marques under one corporate roof offered possibilities the like of which had been beyond the means of either AML or Jaguar alone. The price paid by Ford for Aston Martin was a trifle compared to what they were to be forced to pay for Jaguar, and the fortunes of the Newport Pagnell operation were very much on the back burner as other more pressing imperatives concentrated the attention of the Ford management. For now they were happy to allow the Virage project to go ahead more or less as it had been envisaged.

Suddenly, however, Gauntlett's pet project was also a potential reality. As it turned out, it would evolve not at all in the way he had planned it, but the result was a car that would be hailed (almost) universally as a tour de force. As to whether it was an Aston Martin or not was an entirely different question. Commercial interests said that it was, whereas certain enthusiasts of the flat-earth tendency dismissed it as the XJ7. The reason was the all-too-clear Jaguar connection.

But the Jaguar connection was vital. Whereas the acquisition of Jaguar had been a full-blown campaign,

Walter Hayes

Walter Hayes is on record as saying that if he took the credit for all the things that he is supposed to have done, he would never have had time to do anything. He joined Ford from Fleet Street, where he had been editor of the *Sunday Dispatch*. His rise through Ford's hierarchy was steady and he retired as Vice Chairman of Ford Europe before being called back to the colours over the Aston Martin project.

Walter Hayes (right) with Graham Hill and authors John Blunsden and David Phipps whose book Such Sweet Thunder *tells the story of the Ford F1 engine.*

His input into the development of Cosworth Engineering is well known, as is the role he played in the management of the Ford Advanced Vehicles project, which gave birth to the GT40. His role in the DB7 adventure and his overall strategy for the marque are two primary reasons why the DB7 exists now. As a close friend of Henry Ford II, as well as being his biographer, Hayes's efforts to promote the fortunes of Aston Martin Lagonda were spurred by the untimely death of Ford just as the acquisition was being finalised in 1987.

involving investment bankers, corporate financiers and all the associated moving parts that make up such a large and significant transaction, the Aston Martin affair was rather more the result of a casual conversation between acquaintances, and so, up to a point, the relationship had developed.

It was Hayes's idea to call the proposed DP1999 the DB7. He gathered around him some of the great and the good of competition, such as the splendid Innes Ireland and the tireless Jackie Stewart, and requested, and received, the services of Harry Calton, the veteran Ford PR, to advise on and oversee the process of effectively retro-branding the firm. The Aston Martin Owners' Club, whose influence could not be discounted, were by and large delighted.

The Jaguar acquisition offered Hayes and his colleagues rather more than just a bigger parts bin. In order to develop the idea of DP1999, it was decided to keep the project, for the moment, separate from the Newport Pagnell operations, which were, of course, bringing the Virage to its conclusion and were not ready to be interrupted. But Jaguar had an intimate business relationship with Tom Walkinshaw, the proprietor of TWR, and one of the architects of Jaguar's successful re-entry into sports car racing. Walkinshaw was already engaged in producing the XJ220 model for Jaguar, at a purpose-built site at Bloxham in Oxfordshire, and when that run was over, work could possibly begin on DP1999. At least, that was the theory.

But as the turmoil of the stock market crash receded, the real recession hit. Bolstered by slashed interest rates, the economy soldiered on until 1989, whereupon it started to come unstitched. Demand for cars effectively collapsed. DP1999 rather got lost in the confusion as Ford were forced to indulge in an uncomfortable

amount of short-term rethinking. As professional car-builders and engineers (as well as salesmen), what they had found at Jaguar initially appalled them.

Obviously a hand-built car is low on the list of priorities for a beleaguered businessman; unfortunately, at Newport Pagnell, building of the Virage continued. The late 1980s had, by and large, been kind to them, and domestic demand had been strong, so much so that there was now a Virage line at the old Tickford works on which there were 23 cars at any one time. This was now too much. Hayes and Gauntlett agreed to close the line for a short period and re-evaluate some of the priorities. For the production staff at Newport Pagnell, this involved an unexpected trip to Sweden, to talk to the Volvo production engineers who had made something of a feature of their build method, whereby a single group of workers took each car through its production cycle from start to finish. In this way the simple overhead of a 'line' can be controlled. Henry Ford had always enjoyed a close friendship with Per Gylenhammer, the then chairman of Volvo, and the favour was extended as a matter of course.

At one stage it seemed that the 'new DB4' might never get built, as Europe reeled from the biggest economic shakeout in a quarter of a century. Gauntlett, lowered by the losses with which he felt he was associated, and despite the fact that in the spring of 1988 he had forecast hard times ahead, had other business interests to occupy him and made clear his intention to step down in September 1991. Walter Hayes took his place.

Gauntlett's contribution to the well-being of the firm had been massive; in the minds of the public he had

The DB7's Jaguar-derived supercharged straight-six.

become associated with the marque in almost the same way that Brown had been, and however dismal the business prospects had seemed, his enthusiasm always shone through. He had been honourably reluctant to downscale the works more than necessary during the sales slump. More than anything, by his alliance with Hayes he had ensured the continuity of the marque whatever happened. It does not need an economic genius to speculate what might have happened to Aston Martin Lagonda in the early 1990s without the support of Ford, as more or less its entire market had dried up.

Gauntlett had undertaken to stay three years, and had stayed four; he had kept more or less intact the unique reserves of skill and dedication that were the prime assets of the corporation, and he had found for it a safe and sympathetic pair of hands. No executive could have done more in the circumstances; many in the firm's history had done much less. He is still remembered for the success of his morale-boosting.

Aston Martin was lucky in having the involvement of Hayes. Not only was he a lateral thinker, he had the ear of Ford management and was able to maximise the association in a way that only a skilled corporate insider could. It transpired that the Jaguar management had no particular plans for the Bloxham site – once it was available, perhaps Hayes could find a use for it? He certainly could. He assessed correctly that DP1999 was and only ever had been an idea. There had been no plan to develop the project, as Aston Martin had always lacked the spare development capital necessary for such an effort. Hayes therefore obtained a development budget of £1,000,000 to create a prototype; a chassis was available, that of the venerable but

By now, owners are used to this level of trim – some traditionalists think it soft.

well-handling XJS coupé, which had been the mainstay of Jaguar's sports car production for some 15 years. The car's gothic styling had won it few friends, but all who knew it acknowledged that it was a fine driver's car with an extremely competent chassis.

There was also, potentially, an engine going begging, a 3.2-litre alloy twin-cam straight-six, of XJ40 ancestry rather than XK. The whole specification package was starting to sound right: front engine, steel platform, straight-six engine, alloy coachwork – they were almost there already. A supercharger, a piece of kit dear to Gauntlett's heart, was added. Even better was the fact that Ian Callum, who had been one of the earliest Ford Scholars at the Royal College of Art, was working for TWR on the XJ220 project. He would design it. Once Hayes had got the budget, the go-ahead was given and the prototype was ready in 16 weeks, on time and within budget. Dearborn smiled.

Callum's brief was not to produce a pastiche, and nor did he. What he came up with was to an extent retro-styling, but only in the sense that this is what the DB six-cylinder cars would have evolved into had it not been for the V8 intruding. This was an area where Hayes also had some well-developed ideas. He took the view that Aston Martin had lost its way rather with the V8, and that the DB4-6 cars were the acme of what the firm represented. It was a contentious view, to be sure, but one with which many will concur. Therefore the decision to call the car the DB7, and engage Sir David Brown as President for life was, to put it mildly, well received, not least by Brown himself, who revealed that there may well be a drawerful of DB7 badges lying around at Newport Pagnell; he certainly recollected having some made.

So, by dint of some nifty footwork and a lifetime of contacts, Hayes was

The Aston Martin Owners' Club

Anyone contemplating owning an Aston Martin should consider joining this institution and its associated body, the Aston Martin Heritage Trust. Founded in 1935, it is now a world-wide organisation, dedicated to the promotion, protection, restoration and enjoyment of this most British of marques. Its UK membership is distributed between many areas, each of which has its own area representatives, who co-ordinate the club's activities. Even if you are not a 'joiner', or have been put off car clubs by the grubby-sandwich rivet-counting tendency, the literature alone is well worth the read. The club also supports competitions in the form of hillclimbs, sprints and full race meetings.

The sum total of knowledge represented by the members is vast, and no detail of the history, manufacture, repair and racing of these cars is considered too obscure for detailed consideration. I have drifted in and out of membership over the years and, while I have not exactly been a model member, the club newsletter was always the first thing I opened when it flopped on to the doormat.

Aston Martin Owners' Club
Drayton St. Leonard,
Wallingford,
Oxon OX10 7BG
Tel: 01865 400400
Fax: 01865 400200

The club also maintains a website:
www.amoc.org

Face to face. Despite the interval of over 40 years, the proportions of the DB7 and the DB4 remain pleasingly similar.

able to parlay a tiny budget, wrapped in a vast goodwill, to produce a car that, in his view, the firm should have been making a generation before. He has always been the sort of man for whom people will do things without hesitation. It is an enviable trait. 'Practically everyone I knew wanted to help,' he told me recently; this is, we presume, how Rolls-Royce undertook to paint the cars, for example.

Hayes had established that Ford were prepared to accept lower business margins, but no material losses, on the project, and provided that there was no attempt to re-invent the wheel, significant in-house resources could be applied, and he would be allowed to have some fun. 'Material' was the key word, however. No surprises, please.

But it was rather more than fun. Aston Martin, aside from the DB7 project, and despite their unrivalled

bank of hands-on talent, were critically short of basic resources; for example, the sophisticated test rigs that simulate several million cycles of usage for a given component, such as, literally, bums on seats; and the emission control equipment, which, once used to develop a generation of engines, simply sat around at Dagenham. Aston Martin, by virtue of their new Ford connection, were allowed access to an unprecedented (for them) array of hardware, software and production acumen. But there was more. There were problems.

The recession was having a secondary effect over at Bloxham. The XJ220 was becoming a very slow seller. Since the car had been announced, its specification had been changed somewhat, and this, coupled with the fact that the cars went quickly from premium to discount in the 'pre-owned' market (the list price was in the region of £400,000), triggered something of a buyers' strike. Many held that when they signed up for the car and paid their deposits they had every confidence in expecting a V12 supercar; in reality the engine used was a V6, closely related to the one used in the 6R4 Metro rally car of years before. Jaguar responded by advising them that they should have read the small print. The whole issue got rather unpleasant, and in many ways no one came out of it with huge credit, but the issue was to delay the completion of the XJ220 project and, until it was done, the DB7 had no home.

The DB7, when it was released in 1994, became an instant icon, and significantly has remained so. At first glance it could have been a DB4 Zagato; certainly the clues were there in terms of overall proportions, as well as a few specific design foci and

Released in 1994, the DB7 became an instant icon

visual ratios. Aston Martin, the public reasoned, had produced probably the prettiest car ever built since the last prettiest car ever built, which had also been theirs. Any doubts that Ford had harboured about taking away Jaguar's thunder were immediately assuaged. Queues formed.

As an exercise in brand manipulation, the DB7 was a textbook example of how the motor industry capitalises on its assets. The fact that the DB7 had never been anywhere near Newport Pagnell was irrelevant, for a completely different set of customers emerged who had never shown any particular interest in Aston Martin. That they were ex-Jaguar customers worried Ford not at all, for that in fact is more or less what the customers were buying, but at a substantial premium. Aston Martin immediately

assumed the identity of an up-market Jaguar sports car, leaving Jaguar to concentrate on the development of its 'new E-Type', the XK8, re-enacting the comparisons of the early 1960s between the DB4 and the E-Type Jag.

So, in a sense, Gauntlett also got what he had wanted, even if he was no longer involved – his new DB4. Ford certainly got what they wanted, and a new public took up the debate that had first started at the Geneva show in 1961, but this time the boot was on the other foot. Aston Martin was deemed to be back, with a front-engined twin-cam six-cylinder car that, while expensive, was 'only' in Porsche, as opposed to Virage, territory.

But the DB7 was not to be a volume car as Ford understood it; Hayes advised that a production target of around 600 units a year should be the objective. As the XJS frame had been written down to zero on Jaguar's books years before, certainly there were few doubts that this was an exploitation of free assets, and to an extent the same went for the engine, despite the work that had been done to it to make it deliver, which had been rather more than just strapping on a supercharger.

When the DB7 emerged as a production car, the core values of Callum's design went straight to the solar plexus of all who saw it. It simply looked right. Whereas the 'appointments' of the Aston Martin range, with a few exceptions in the 1980s (and the Lagonda), had focused on the functional, the interior of the DB7, styled by Neil Simpson, Callum's colleague at TWR, was both cosy and opulent.

Very few women, for example, had been fans of the marque up to now, except perhaps to look at. The V8s were far too macho and the six-cylinder models had all required considerable heft (as well as a certain 1950s mindset) to drive smoothly. The DB7 changed all that. It made the

marque accessible. Dearborn smiled even more…

As to those who were narrow-eyed about the car being a re-invented XJS, then a drive in it seduced them. It was clearly rather more than a recycled chassis, a pretty body and a strapped-on blower; the re-engineering that had gone on had produced a vehicle that people simply wanted to own. Thus the decision to limit production was a hard one to take, but even so it has outsold any other Aston yet made.

All Hayes's assumptions about the role that small groups can play within a larger corporate whole were proved to be correct with the management of the DB7 project. From 1913 up until this point, Aston Martin had, as a marque, between all its owners, investors and engineers, produced something like half an hour's worth of production in Detroit terms. The impact of the DB7 did not exactly transform the parent company, of course, and indeed that was not the main intention, but the cross-fertilisation process of ideas and themes has clearly accelerated. At last, Aston Martin had serious investment behind it.

It was not long before uprated versions of the DB7 were mooted. The first of these was the DB7 Volante which lost little of the elegant smoothness of its saloon counterpart. The 'original' DB7 GT was a good example, originally intended for a one-make racing series. Three were built, but the momentum for the venture never took off and they are all in private hands. A V8-engined DB7 almost qualified for the Le Mans race in 1994 but was, ironically, pipped at the post by a Lister. Shades of 1957.

While it was clear that the DB7 was a very fine and competent car (the sales figures rather suggested that) and infinitely better from a visual point of view than its Jaguar progen-

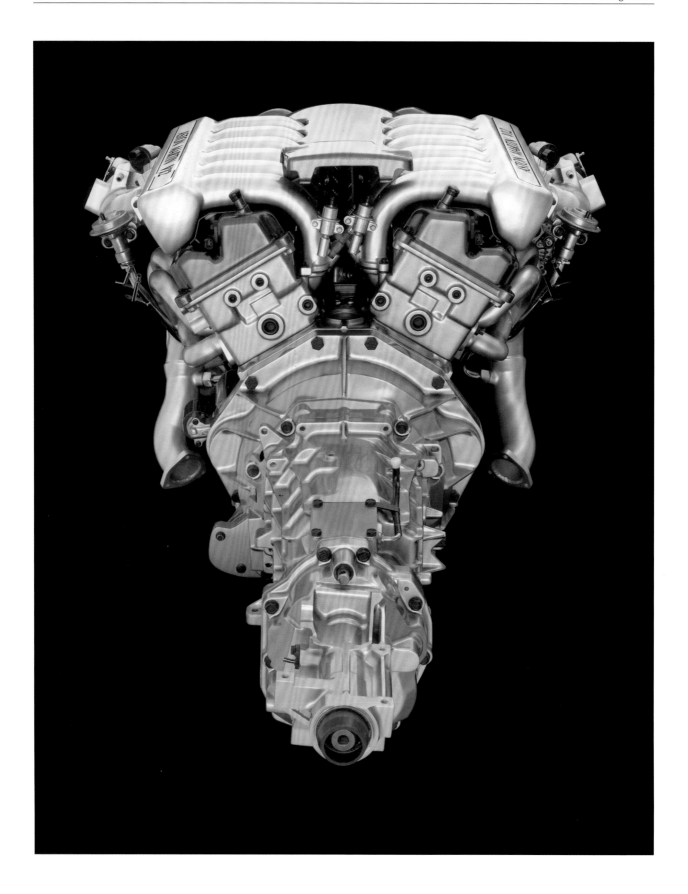

Aston Martin DB7 Vantage

ENGINE:
All-alloy quad overhead cam 48-valve 5,935cc V12. Compression ratio 10.3:1. Visteon EEC V engine management controlling fuel injection, ignition and diagnostics. Fully catalysed stainless steel exhaust system

TRANSMISSION:
Six-speed manual with optional five-speed automatic. Limited slip differential Ratio 3.77:1 (man) 3.06:1 (auto)

STEERING:
Rack and pinion, power-assisted 2.54 turns lock to lock. Column tilt and reach adjustment

SUSPENSION:
Front: Independent double wishbone incorporating anti-dive geometry. Coil springs, monotube dampers and anti-roll bar
Rear: Independent double wishbone incorporating longitudinal control arms, coil springs, monotube dampers and anti-roll bar

BRAKES:
Front: Ventilated cross-drilled steel discs 355mm diameter with alloy four-piston calipers
Rear: Ventilated steel discs 330mm diameter with alloy four-piston calipers and drum handbrake. Teves anti-lock braking activation system (ABS)

WHEELS AND TYRES:
Unique lightweight aluminium alloy wheels 8J x 18 (front), 9J x 18 (rear) Bridgestone SO2 245/40 ZR18 tyres (front), 265/35 (rear)

BODYWORK:
Two door coupé or convertible body style with 2+2 seating. Steel underframe and body panels. Composite front wings, sills, boot lid and front and rear bumpers/aprons. Side impact protection in doors. Boot space of 0.178cu m (6.14cu ft)

INTERIOR:
Full Connolly leather interior. Electrically controlled front seats incorporating seat heaters. Air conditioning, rear screen and mirror heating, electronic traction control. Six-speaker Kenwood stereo radio cassette system with CD autochanger. Alarm and immobiliser system with remote central locking and trunk release

LENGTH: 4.66m (15ft 2in)

WIDTH: 1.83m (5ft 11½in)

WHEELBASE: 2.59m (8ft 5in)

HEIGHT: Coupé 1.24m (4ft 0¼in), Volante 1.26m (4ft 1in)

KERB WEIGHT: Coupé 1,780kg (35.04cwt), Volante 1,875kg (36.91cwt)

FUEL TANK CAPACITY:
Coupé 89l (19.6gal), Volante 82l (18.0gal), 95 RON unleaded fuel only

MAX POWER: 309kW (420bhp) @ 6,000rpm

MAX TORQUE: 540Nm (400lb ft) @ 5,000rpm

ACCELERATION: 0–100kph (62mph) 5.0 seconds (manual transmission)

MAX SPEED: Coupé 298kph (185mph), Volante 266kph (165mph)

WEIGHT:	33.9cwt (1,723kg)
MAX SPEED:	165mph (265kph)
PRICE NEW:	£78,000

The splendid Aston Martin V12 unit.

itor, the veteran chassis which formed its basis had, of course, been designed to accept a V12 engine; and while the magnificent Jaguar V12 unit was now both too long in the tooth and too politically incorrect to be useful, the proven 6-litre V12 unit was available, which had been proposed for use in the 1993 Lagonda Vignale prototype, and the then-mooted project Vantage.

There was, of course, nothing wrong with the blown six-cylinder engine either; in service it had proved reliable enough and quite powerful, but experiments with the V12 when installed in the 'original' DB7 GT for the purpose of an abortive single-marque racing programme had delivered a car of startling ability.

The all-alloy 48-valve unit produced 400bhp from just less than six litres, or about 67bhp per litre, which, given the only modest difference in weight between the 3.2-litre six and the new

V12, offered a useful boost in power-to-weight ratio as well as rationalising engine production schedules – which, at the time of writing, are decamping to Cologne. The DB7 was thus transformed, from a worthy machine which sold on its looks as much as anything, to a purposeful device which firmly attacked its target market.

Naturally, the car looks the part, with a host of tiny modifications, most of which concern driver comfort, although the upgrading of the brakes is, after the appreciable difference in engine output, probably the most satisfying element of the new package. For those who were brought up in David Brown Aston Martins, the Brembo braking system, assisted by ABS (Teves), is a revelation. For those tolerating, by today's standards slippery Dunlop or Girling discs, let alone shuddering, squealing Al-fin drums, modern brakes are a revelation.

All in all, this car makes a simple point; Aston Martin just could not

have done it on their own. Whereas the last all-new car designed under the independent company, the Virage, had been a worthy if disappointing machine, what is clear about this new generation of cars is the simple attention to technical detail the result of that commercial leisure time which is unimaginable to a small builder. Imagine a Morgan built by Mazda, so to speak: what is initially a charming idiosyncrasy becomes a true nuisance when compared with the smoothed and streamlined product that results from the serious application of R&D. There is no doubt that with the DB7 Vantage, this new generation came of age, particularly given that the tuning possibilities of the relatively unstressed engine are obvious.

There is a downside to this for a DB7 owner, though. It would be foolish to pretend that the original six-cylinder car is anything like as desirable as the V12, to the point where I can imagine that the first series of cars are, as I

Familiar, but radically different under the bonnet.

Not all cars are comfortable as convertibles; this is an exception.

write, starting to find their way into the hands of 'non-specialist' dealers – our cheery psychopaths. This may be a matter of profound regret, but underscores the simple fact that nothing stays still for long.

For those traditionalists by whom the DB7 was seen to be something of a hybrid Jaguar, the introduction of the V12 engine went some, but not all the way, towards reassuring them that the resurgence of the marque was not merely a flash in the pan. Many had forgotten that the cherished DB2 was in fact the amalgamation of an existing chassis with an existing engine clothed in a body of startling beauty. Apart from the fact that the DB7 (with whatever engine) thus represents a process which is both old and honourable, it is also an extremely fine car. The fact that the chassis behaves with much more composure than it ever did when carrying a Jaguar body should not be lost upon them.

The DB7 GT is perhaps illogically named. It is a DB7 Vantage, but more so. A tweaked engine (435bhp) is part of it, but brakes which are closer to Vanquish specification are also included, as well as a quicker final drive of 4.09:1. The transmission (a choice between six-speed manual or five-speed automatic) has yet to approach the sophistication of the device used on the Vanquish, but probably it does not need to. The most significant revisions, though, are to the aerodynamics of the underbody, which serve to reduce lift by an astonishing 50 per cent (which rather begs the question, I suppose...), as well as extensive changes to damping, wishbones, and spring rates. The GT thus offers a harder ride than the Vantage, but such is the level of internal cosseting (the only element of these cars at which I bridle somewhat) that the driver barely notices. The indirect gear acceleration is as astonishing now as it was to the early testers of

Above: The DB7 GT benefits from a tweaked V12 engine, sports suspension, and improved underbody aerodynamics.

Below: Styling studies for the DB7 Zagato reflected hints of the 1950s and 1970s . . .

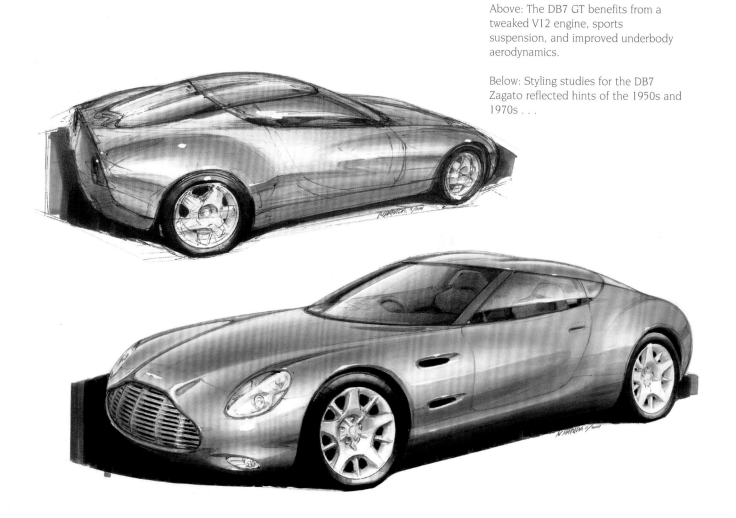

the original DB4, which is exactly the point.

And the noise is wonderful. An effective device (also fitted to the Vanquish), and one which in its conception recalls the Continental Rolls-Royce, is a silencer by-pass valve, which reduces exhaust back pressure at higher revs. One gets the full sensation when speeding through a tunnel in third gear. There is little doubt in my mind that these V12s are the best sounding Aston Martins since the DB Mark III.

The gorgeous DB7 Zagato is based on the DB7 Vantage, as if the structural specification had changed significantly, the 'new' design would have been required to undergo the rigourous and costly process of crash testing. Another interpretation

is that if a shorter DB7 was to be built, then it was always going to be difficult to interfere with Ian Callum's core design, particularly by this much. The result might have merely looked odd rather than advanced. In the days of the DB4GT, modification to a chassis – no two of which were exactly alike – was merely a matter of metal bashing. Now that things are a little more sophisticated, it made eminent sense for an outside coachbuilder to have a go.

The result is, as one might expect, stunning, the prettiest car, in fact, since the original Zagato DB4GT and a long way removed from the previous Aston to wear that badge. The DB7 Vantage Volante chassis, on which the car is based, is shortened by a mere 60mm, but body overhang

is reduced by 127mm at the rear and 24mm at the front, which has the effect of visually shortening the car by rather a lot. Because it was only ever going to be a two-seater there is no appreciable loss of accommodation inside – indeed, by comparison with a standard four-seater DB7 it is relatively roomy.

There are hints of retro-styling about the Zagato, but it is none the worse for that. The gaping grille recalls Touring's Lancia Flaminia of 40 years ago, from the same portfolio which delivered the DB4. At the time of writing there are no performance figures available, but suffice it to say that it will in all probability be as fast or faster than the Vantage. It would be rather silly if it were not, although once a car has the attributes of the DB7 Vantage, anything more is rather academic, as I found out with the original V8 Vantage.

The bodywork of this extremely important car is built more or less traditionally. The roof is steel, the body panels hand-worked aluminium alloy, the sill covers and front and rear aprons made from composites. All-up weight, at 1,740kg (34.25cwt), is 60kg lighter than the original DB7 Vantage Volante. All in all, a delicious prospect, but one to which very few of us can look forward, and not merely because of the price. The limited number to be made (99) will, barring a global economic meltdown, ensure a certain measure of exclusivity.

For a Zagato execution, the design is remarkably uncontroversial, and, when compared to the last offering from that company to wear an Aston Martin badge, utterly beguiling. It is obviously an Aston, and not merely because all other supercars (Jaguar aside) seem to have their engines in the back. The more I look at it, the lovelier it is. It has been a long time since I have been able to say that in all honesty.

Naturally, because it is at heart a DB7 it is not perfect, and not entirely because it is hand-made, either. The dynamics of the DB7 platform are tautened by even this modest amount of shortening and the stiffening necessary to produce a convertible body add even further strength. Typical of the thoroughness with which Aston Martin have always addressed suspension and steering, the result has been described as one of the best-sorted front-engined

sports cars around, quite irrespective of the elegance of its coachwork.

Looking forward, I can well imagine that this car might be The One; if there are any car collectors around in 40 years time (or, more critically, if there is any petrol), the DB7 Zagato will be the icon over which grown men who are currently schoolboys will drool. We can imagine tasteful reproductions of it; 'tribute' cars, as the motor trade quaintly calls them; our cheery psychopath may yet take a hacksaw to that unsold six-cylinder LWB DB7 in his warehouse, steam clean an oily lump from an XJ12 and heave it in. Even cheaper, cut and shut ratty old XJSs instead. Worse things have happened to E-types, after all. In all seriousness, I predict a minor new sub-marque developing around this car (and extremely nasty it will be, too) as the arc-welders and cutting torches strobe Sarf London railway arches to the descant wail of Pavarotti and the odour of curing glass fibre and singed sheepskin. 'Inspirin', innit?'

I will expand this theme no further, save to observe that examples of the XJS are appropriately inexpensive at the time of writing.

From the sublime to the dubious. The Aston Martin David Brown American Roadster (Mark 1) is not, as you might imagine, merely a drophead version of the DB7 Zagato, for the simple reason that it has no roof at all, nothing, not even a few sticks and a bit of canvas. Neither is it a competition car, despite the faint suggestion of that implied by the name as well as the hint of fairings behind the heads of the occupants. Neither, I may add, is it envisioned selling it in anything other than left-hand drive, which is a shame for the Antipodes. Or not, depending on your point of view. It is perhaps a good example of the oft-encountered phenomenon, that a roofless version of a beautiful car is seldom as pretty as the original. But as tanning machines go, it is surely extraordinary enough. It is also pretty enough, until you compare it to the Zagato-bodied coupé from whence it came.

I do not dislike it that much; I have no doubt it is as fine a car as its progenitor. I do bridle at the almost coy pastiche styling details, though, which seem to hark back to the DBR racers (a bit) and rather remind me of some of the stylistic bogosties found on early Ford Mustangs. All the same, I hope they sell lots of them; it's just that I rather hope they all stay in America, which, barring extensive and rapid global warming, they probably will. One plus is that they are available in manual 'change only, but I can only imagine that in the target market, which I assume is California, that limitation will not persist. As will be seen here, the specification is very similar to the car from which it is derived, the DB7 Vantage Volante. So new is this car, though, that at the time of writing we do not know its exact dimensions.

So, welcome to the new Aston Martins. Certainly they will not be to everyone's taste – this is not a marque which is everyone's cup of tea, after all – but given that that the front engine, rear-wheel-drive layout has become holy writ for Aston Martin cars, then I cannot think of any particular in which the current crop 'lets the side down' whatsoever. Anyone who has followed the fortunes of the company, particularly in the last generation, will realise that it is something of a miracle (mainly, it must be said, the original determination of Victor Gauntlett) that it exists at all. That it exists in the state it does, and is capable of producing cars as well thought-out and executed as these are, is the result of an unspoken conspiracy between the owner of the company and the owners of the cars.

The DBAR I, aimed at the US market, is derived from the Zagato coupé. The car is a true roadster, completely devoid of weather equipment.

DBAR 1

ENGINE:
All-alloy quad overhead cam 48-valve 5,935cc V12. Compression ratio 10.3:1. Visteon EEC V engine management controlling fuel injection, ignition and diagnostics. Fully catalysed stainless steel bypass valve exhaust system

TRANSMISSION:
Six-speed manual. Limited slip differential. Ratio 4.09:1

STEERING:
Rack and pinion, power-assisted 2.54 turns lock to lock. Column tilt and reach adjustment

SUSPENSION:
Front: Independent double wishbone incorporating anti-dive geometry. Coil springs, monotube dampers and anti-roll bar
Rear: Independent double wishbone incorporating longitudinal control arms, coil springs, monotube dampers and anti-roll bar

BRAKES:
Front: Ventilated grooved steel discs 355mm diameter with alloy four-piston calipers
Rear: Ventilated grooved steel discs 330mm diameter with alloy four-piston calipers and drum handbrake. Teves anti-lock braking activation system (ABS)

WHEELS AND TYRES:
Multispoke lightweight aluminium wheels 8J x 19 (front), 9½J x 19 (rear). Yokohama SO2 245/40 ZR19 tyres (front), 265/35 (rear)

BODYWORK:
Two-door, with 2+0 seating. Steel underframe and body panels. Aluminium front wings, sills, boot lid with integral spoiler and front and rear bumpers/aprons. Side impact protection in doors

INTERIOR:
Bridge of Weir leather interior. Electrically controlled sports front seats incorporating optional seat heaters. Electronic traction control. Six-speaker Becker stereo radio cassette system with 6 disc CD autochanger. Alarm and immobiliser system with remote central locking and trunk release

MAX POWER: 435bhp (324kW) @ 6,000rpm (manual only)

MAX TORQUE: 556Nm (410lb ft) @ 5,000rpm (manual only)

ACCELERATION: 0–100kph (62mph) under 5.0 seconds (manual only)

MAX SPEED: Approx 185mph (298kph) (manual only)

PRICE NEW: £78,000

Aston Martin *'V' cars*

The contemporary
Aston Martin Vantage.

During the early months and years of the Ford association, when a series of astonished business school graduates came away from Newport Pagnell almost crying at the inefficiency of it all, Hayes determined that exposure and access to the little firm should be controlled. As the business climate picked up, this was easier and easier to do, but in a sense a curtain was draped around the activities of Aston Martin. There were things that needed doing, but in private; not the least of these was a redesign of the Virage, starting with its name – from now on, the big Astons were just known as 'V' cars.

It is unusual, to say the least, to find a front-engined road car capable of 190mph (306kph). Machines with mid or rear engines of similar calibre are, if not exactly two a penny, hardly unobtainable. The main reason for this is weight, as the grand prix world discovered when Charles Cooper introduced the first of his line of mid-engined racing cars.

The benefits of the mid- or rear-engine layout can be summed up in terms of weight and traction. The weight savings are huge: the massive propshaft can go, and with it the weight of the rigid structure to support it. The individual transmission components can also be lighter, as the gearbox/axle that drives the wheels can rely on the mass of the engine to support it, and with that the structure of the front of the car can be redesigned to support only steering, brakes and tankage. Better traction, less weight, better power-to-weight ratio – and so it goes on, until you end up with a racing car.

The 'V' cars benefited from access to Ford funding and R&D

But such cars are invariably two-seaters, or in the case of the McLaren, three. The Virage had hardly been a family saloon, but it was at least capable of seating four. It was also supremely attractive, and people liked it, but they were not moved by it in the way that they had been by, say, the Zagato, or the DB4GT, or even the DBSV8. It was a good car, but despite its undeniable beauty, it broke no new ground in terms of performance, and the handling was in many ways inferior to its predecessor. All in all, it was a bit of a let-down.

Only a few cars even try to adhere to the 'traditional' front-engine layout and attempt to approach the speeds of which the modern generation of 'supercars' is capable: the Dodge Viper, the Lister Storm (actually mid-front-engined), the Bentley and the Aston Martin Vantage. They are all in many ways magnificent anachronisms, but it is pleasing that they exist.

But if Aston Martin had lost its way after the DB6, which was Hayes's view, the core product of the firm, the Virage, should really be allowed to benefit from the association with Ford in a meaningful way. It was no good developing a range of costly

benchmark automobiles if the core of the development was taking place outside the factory, on the racetrack with the privately funded AMRs, or at Richard Williams's workshop, or even at the Wiscombe Park hillclimb or the Curborough sprint, with comically overdeveloped specials, splendid though all agreed they were. This was not product.

The Vantage, painted in its evocative Aston Martin racing green.

Reeves Callaway's brief had been to allow for further development using forced induction. Here it was. The application of two superchargers to the four-valve V8 produced, with a sensibly lowered compression ratio, a reliable 550bhp with 550lb ft of torque. Drive-by-noise rules mandate the use of a six-speed transmission, so that engine rpm is kept low, but that can be changed, post-registration.

Where the new range of 'V' cars has a distinct edge is in the field of engine management. Gone is the Weber/Marelli fuel system, now replaced by the Ford-sourced EEC IV engine management package, which in effect treats the big V8 as two four-cylinder units. The stated Vantage engine output of 550bhp

and 550lb ft of torque is produced at 6,500 and 3,000rpm respectively, and is in fact probably rather more than that. And there is still something left.

The Virage had already been through a few stages of development; the use of a 6.3-litre engine, already proven by ex-factory developers to be quite tractable, was the first mechanical adjustment, with body modifications to match, and it was indeed a great improvement over the first cars, producing a mighty 500bhp with relatively little trouble. The adjustable suspension was a major step forward and the car was brutally quick, but as a production prospect it was limited, and even made the standard Virage look a little silly.

Even with precise measuring, no two Aston Martins are the same. (Aston Martin Lagonda)

The Vantage, though, was different, despite its external resemblance to the Heffernan/Greenley design of the previous model. The car shared the same wheelbase of its predecessors with the Beach chassis, and indeed all the other major proportions, but the whole structure was extensively lightened and, most significantly, the triangular rear A-frame, which had caused the bother at the launch of the Virage, was dispensed with. It was replaced with a sturdy development of the axle location as used on the last of the V8 Vantage saloons. The result was a lighter platform with much less rear end compliance. It was the most radical redesign that the Harold Beach chassis had undergone and no one was particularly surprised when it was realised how much it could be lightened without compromising its integrity.

It is relatively easy to build softly sprung cars, as generations of Detroit designers will attest. Harder is the challenge to produce a well-sprung car with the minimum of suspension compliance, so that the loads that are exerted on each corner of the car can be controlled, not by the inexactitudes of masses of rubber, vast leaf springs or compressed air, but by engineering precision. Very few manufacturers have managed to accomplish it with any degree of success. Drive the worst sports car in the world, the Corvette – that classically vulgar example of power without responsibility – and experience what I mean.

The ability to engineer a large car, particularly a front-engined one, so that it is fast and can (if necessary) be steered and braked at the same time

From the DB2 to the Vantage, this is the way Aston Martins are made. (Aston Martin Lagonda)

The interior is basically similar to that of the Virage.

while remaining comfortable, has always been the biggest challenge, and Aston Martin, like Bristol, have always been contenders for the laurels. Such a task is usually the remit of the small manufacturer, so the cars are invariably costly. To the driver of a 'muscle car', which will merely outdrag most other machines, the Aston Martin marque is a puzzle – they can always make it go faster, so why don't they? Well, they always do, but it is also a feature of these cars that no quicker version of an existing model has ever had handling that is inferior to its predecessor, even though it is invariably more powerful. The exact choice of words here is necessary if only to let the DB5 off the hook, which was only technically a

new model, and really an exception to the rule and thus a minor aberration.

The Vantage, and its siblings the V8 coupé and the Volante, are logical developments of the theme started with the DBS, but due to their lighter weight and developed engines and transmissions, they are superior in almost all departments. Some consider them to be over-trimmed, but if that is what the market wants, then so be it. The history books are full of car companies who tried to buck the market and failed.

Naturally, if the customer wants it, virtually anything can be created, provided it has five wheels and an engine; for example, if you want a shooting brake, they will make one for you, although they do not qualify as fast sellers. More normal fare, DB7 aside, and generally built to order, is the V8 coupé, offering a modest 350bhp, the Volante, power output the same, and the Vantage, delivering its whopping 550bhp.

So in a sense the 'V' cars are both a logical development of the Virage as well as being a major re-invention of it. The pleasing proportions of the design are not lost, and the mechanical accomplishments are several degrees better, permitted by the unprecedented access that AML has had to the Ford research and development facilities. The cars are still recognisably Aston Martin V8s, but have benefited hugely from a financial input from Ford that is relatively small by the standards of the investor, but colossal by the standards of the recipient. In reality,

of course, it was a skilled exploitation of existing resources on a benign basis, but the results have set new standards for the class of car. Naturally, there will be more to come.

So, at Newport Pagnell gone now is the 23-car line, replaced in part by a quite staggering restoration and service facility, alongside a bespoke production facility for the 'V' cars. The restoration facilities offered by the service department under the direction of Kingsley Riding-Felce are enviably comprehensive, and, it should be said, not in the bargain basement in terms of price. But in the context of the 'car for life' theme launched by Walter Hayes in 1991, the owner can call upon the services of a unique group of people, many of whom will have played a role in building the car in the first place.

A stem-to-stern rebuild is no light undertaking, but despite the fact that the marque is as popular now as it has ever been, one might imagine that there was a finite supply of cars that might require it. Apparently not.

The twin-supercharged Callaway-Marek engine.

Project Vantage: into the new Millennium

The Project Vantage was first seen in 1998 – originally a one-off prototype to indicate the future direction of Aston Martin. At first glance a DB7 on steroids, in reality it was rather more radical than that. The resemblance to the DB4GT Zagato was even more marked, but in that the car was designed by Ian Callum it was only superficially a DB7 derivative. With an extruded alloy and composite chassis and alloy outer body, powered by a 450bhp 6-litre V12 with a Formula 1-style paddle gearchange, the Project Vantage was theoretically capable of over 200mph (322kph), not least because it was almost 1,000kg (19.7cwt) lighter than the current AM Vantage and, despite its appearance, not that much smaller.

The engine we had seen before. It was the 48-valve alloy-blocked unit that was mooted to power the aborted Lagonda Vignale. Although the output was relatively modest, at 450bhp, the target weight for the car suggested that a 0–60mph (97kph) time would be in the order of 4 seconds.

The interior was a visual delight of brushed alloy, leather and carbon fibre; it marked a reassessment of the opulence found in the V8 cars and, of course, also contributed to the proposed weight savings. All in all, it was a mouthwatering prospect.

Project Vantage received an enthusiastic welcome, and the brave decision was taken to develop the concept for production as the Vanquish. After last-minute changes to various styling details, at the insistence of newly appointed Aston Martin CEO Ulrich Bez, the Vanquish was unveiled at the 2001 Geneva Salon.

The proposed interior of the Project Vantage, with its extensive use of high tech materials was a departure, but most would agree that it worked rather well.

(All Aston Martin Lagonda)

Left top:
Project Vantage. Another triumph for Ian Callum, this one-off V12-powered car bears a superficial resemblance to the DB7, but in the flesh it is Vantage-sized, while retaining some of the proportions of the smaller car. The lineage is clear and reflects the original inspiration – Zagato. Like the DB7, it is a clever development of the theme but is entirely original in its execution.

Left bottom:
The side view of the Project. The tail in particular echoes the Kamm design first seen on the project cars and the DB6. Note the trademark air vent, without which no Aston Martin would be complete.

The appellation 'Works prepared', which is the service department's seal of approval on a restoration or modification, will probably, over time, come to constitute a benchmark by which all such efforts are judged. It was not always so, it must be said, and the repositioning of the factory service effort has, under Riding-Felce, provided a much-needed safe haven for owners world-wide, not that they are exactly stranded at the moment: Aston Martin has always enjoyed as a marque a higher proportion of dedicated specialists per car built than any other manufacturer, and, as one of them put it to me, the factory has no excuse not to stock the relevant parts now. In the past, that was not always so.

As well as the restoration facilities, the special tuning options for the fortunate owners of both 'V' cars and the DB series are bewildering. Whereas the 'Works prepared' process exists for the uprating of older cars, the 'Driving Dynamics' packages available for all current cars include

both power and handling tweaks to satisfy the most demanding. A 600bhp engine for your Vantage? No problem. A five-speed transmission? Likewise. It seems a shocking waste to remove a six-speed box and replace it with a five-speed, but it does sharpen up the Vantage a little, at the expense of passers-by. Similarly, AP racing brakes can be fitted so that your 600bhp monster can pull up smartly. All this is horrendously costly, of course, but several dozen owners have opted for it.

A visit to the Aston Martin works at Newport Pagnell now is a very different experience from a few short years ago. Everywhere the evidence of major investment leaps out, but without the essence of the place being lost. It is still pleasingly quiet, although not for reasons of a slack market; the last time I had been there was in 1991 in the teeth of a recession, and even though Ford were in charge the auguries were not that wonderful. Back again, one is immediately struck by the feeling that here are people doing what they are supremely good at, supported, at long last, by levels of capital that allow them to do it. There were some doubting Thomases at the time of the Ford takeover, I well remember. I had no particular view, but it occurs to me that while I still do not regard the Aston Martin as the Englishman's Ferrari, I think it is safe to say that it is certainly Ford's Ferrari.

Whatever they produce next, whether it is an even more outrageous development of the stunning Vanquish, a DB9 variant or something totally different, it is clear that to the people who actually make them, it will probably make little difference. To the man with the clipboard scheduling the day's restoration agenda at Newport Pagnell, repairing a dent is repairing a dent, and if the prospect of carbon fibre composites upsets him, he doesn't show it. I cannot imagine what Mr Goldstone would make of it all.

In the first edition of this book, I speculated as to whether the Vanquish would actually go into production; well, dear reader, it did, and an extraordinary thing it is, too. For the first time in its history, Aston Martin has produced a car which does significantly more than it needs to. In fact, in terms of flagship models, the Vanquish is the most significant event since the DB4 and completely new in all respects. Remarkably, it is almost indistinguishable from its prototype; a statement of confidence if ever there was one.

Conceptually, it is familiar to us, of course – a front-engined road burner with a marked family resemblance to the DB7. But after that the differences are clear. The engine, the 48-valve twin cam V12, displacing 6 litres, is also now found in the DB7 of course (in a slightly milder state of tune), but even the Vanquish probably has further potential, provided that the owner has a developed view about what to do with it once it has been fettled.

The main departure from familiar ground is found in the chassis. There

Below: The Vanquish uses an extruded aluminium/carbon fibre/composite monocoque.

Right: Simply stunning, from any angle. Hand-fitted Vanquish bodywork is close to perfection.

■ **Carbon Fibre/Composite materials**

isn't one. Finally, the splendid (but much-modified) Harold Beach-inspired platform layout is constructed from extruded aluminium sections, bonded and riveted to a central spine which is a rigid carbon fibre transmission tunnel.

Whereas previous Aston Martins all contained various components which could have been spare parts for a World War 2 battleship, the Vanquish replaces vast amounts of this ferrous metal with a similar volume of aluminium, carbon fibre, and composites. The weight-saving is actually less than one would imagine, as the all-up weight of the car is 1,835kg (36.1cwt), actually a little more than its predecessor. But the engineering is exquisite. The precision offered by the use of advanced materials as compared to steel fabrications ensures a greater uniformity than ever before. The

observable differences between one car and another are now a thing of the past. Whisper it, though: panels might well be fully interchangeable.

And yet, it still takes five hours to fettle an alloy wing panel to fit, the objective being as close to perfection as human agency can deliver. It succeeds, too. The Vanquish is as visually perfect in the execution of its bodywork as the use of aluminium alloy will allow, and not merely because of the eight coats of paint, either. As with all Aston Martins before it, there is no filler, none. The very idea of such sloppy inexactitude makes lips curl with derision at both Newport Pagnell and Bloxham. As before, one may argue the merits of an Aston Martin against its commercial opposition, but one thing remains clear: these cars are probably better-built than anything else on the road, with the possible exception of a Bristol, which I could

imagine I. K. Brunel admiring but probably not R. J. Mitchell.

The transmission is the car's most obvious other technical feature, being a device developed in conjunction with Magnetti Marelli. Unsurprisingly, given that connection, it is electro-hydraulic, and operated, racing style, by paddles on the obverse of the steering wheel. It takes a little getting used to and is not the easiest device to master, particularly in heavy traffic. Needless to say, the management of all this power (about 460bhp) is going to need something fairly massive and there is no doubt that the transmission is beefy enough to take it. Happily, though, a relatively short stroke V12 is never going to generate the stump-pulling torque of a supercharged V8, even though peak power is achieved at a relatively mild 6,500rpm. I have no doubt that work has already started somewhere to

'liberate' more power from this splendid engine.

But the Vanquish is more than merely a pretty car with a clever gearbox. Although the overall weight and dimensions are not exactly foreign to the marque's flagship range (a quick comparison with the last V8 Vantage reveals this), the balance of the car is completely altered, by virtue of the materials from which it is built, as well as the distribution of the engine and transmission.

For 'the enthusiast', however, what is a virtue in a new car will surely be an insurmountable obstacle for a restorer in years to come. It will be some time before these vehicles trickle down in price to the level at which they are 'affordable', and I cannot seriously imagine our cheery psychopath ever making a market in them, so the Vanquish, for the moment, will remain parked firmly on the pinnacle where it now sits. In fact, in the universe of 'supercars', to which the Vanquish surely belongs, it may even be something of a bargain.

It is also, of course, the James Bond car of the new century. Never mind that the engine and transmission had to be discarded in order to insert the various gadgets and special effects; the sight of 007 back behind the wheel of a proper car, particularly one made at Newport Pagnell, served to gladden the hearts of many – a good example of the law of unintended consequences, and surely one of the best global public relations undertakings ever.

England's finest: 007's 'special equipment' Vanquish on the set of *Die Another Day*.

V12 Vanquish
2001 to date

ENGINE:
All-alloy twin overhead cam 48 valve 5,935cc 60° V12. Compression ratio 10.5:1. Visteon twin PTEC engine management controlling fuel injection, ignition and diagnostics. Fully catalysed stainless steel exhaust system

TRANSMISSION:
Six-speed manual gearbox with Auto Shift Manual/Select Shift Manual (ASM/SSM) electro-hydraulic control system. SCP/CAN interface to engine management control system. Limited slip differential 3.69:1

STEERING:
Rack and pinion, variable power assistance 2.73 turns lock to lock. Column tilt and reach adjustment

SUSPENSION:
Front: Independent double aluminium wishbone. Coil springs, monotube damper and anti-roll bar
Rear: Independent double aluminium wishbone. Coil springs, monotube damper and anti-roll bar

BRAKES:
Front: Ventilated cross-drilled steel discs 355mm diameter with four piston service caliper
Rear: Ventilated steel discs 330mm diameter with four piston service caliper and separate handbrake caliper. Teves vacuum assisted anti-lock braking system. Electronic brake and engine intervention traction control system

WHEELS AND TYRES:
Lightweight forged aluminium alloy wheels 9J x 19 (front), 10J x 19 (rear) Yokohama 255/40 ZR19 tyres (front), 285/40 ZR19 (rear)

BODYWORK:
Two door style with 2+0 or 2+2 seating. Extruded aluminium and carbon fibre bonded monocoque. Composite front and rear crash structures. Aluminium skin panels. Extruded aluminium door side impact protection beam. Blade mounted washer jets. Boot space of 0.24cu m (8.48cu ft)

INTERIOR:
Connolly (now Bridge of Weir) leather and Alcantara interior. Electrically controlled front seats incorporating seat heaters. Air conditioning. Heated rear screen. Six-speaker Alpine stereo radio cassette system with 6 CD autochanger. Alarm and immobiliser system with remote central locking and boot release. Tyre pressure sensing system. Automatic rain sensing wiper operation. Automatic headlamp operation. Auto dimming rear view mirror. Trip computer. Instrument pack message centre display. Battery disconnect switch

LENGTH: 4.66m (15ft 2in)

WIDTH: 1.92m (6ft 3in)

WHEELBASE: 2.69m (8ft 9in)

HEIGHT: 1.32m (4ft 3½in)

KERB WEIGHT: 1,835kg (36.12cwt)

FUEL TANK CAPACITY: 80l (17.6gal), 95 RON unleaded fuel only

MAX POWER: 343kW (460bhp) @ 6,500rpm

MAX TORQUE: 542Nm (400lb ft) @ 5,000rpm

ACCELERATION: 0–100kph (62mph) 5.0 seconds

MAX SPEED: 306kph (190mph)

Aston Martin
DB9

For the traditionalists who had surveyed the DB7 with something less than unalloyed pleasure, and who took great pleasure in pointing out that it was the car that the Jaguar XJS should have been, there were moments of confusion about the next direction the company's products would take. Quite revealing was the fact that very few owners of pre-Ford Aston Martins saw fit to exchange their DB4s for DB7s, for example, despite the fact that our cheery psychopath was starting to get his string-backed grip around quite a few of them by the end of 2001 – only to find, like many, that the DB7 was perhaps merely a

rather well laid-out and pretty Jag (a car which was no better than it should have been), and that some of the detailing was, to his surprise, rather familiar, particularly some of the rather naff (Mazda sourced) switchgear.

When Ulrich Bez arrived at Aston Martin in mid-2000 he was slightly dismayed to note that the major project in hand was a mid-engined V8. It had been designed (by Ian Callum) and signed off (by Jac Nasser) and was all ready. Bez was troubled by this: 'Ferrari can do a mid-engined car, because it's been doing them for 40 years,' he commented in October 2003, 'but

DB9: interestingly, the rear pillar is pure DB5; the rest is rather more avant garde.

not Aston Martin.' He had a point. The tortuous evolution of the modern mid-engine sports car offers so many traps for the unwary that even the masters get it wrong occasionally – try throwing an early Ferrari 365 BB around too hard to see what I mean – and it might even have looked a little 'me too, please'. Given that his impeccable engineering background included Porsche, whose resurgence as a front-engined car builder had paid vast dividends, he knew of what he spoke, and, in those vital first months (after which a new boss enjoys a fast closing window of opportunity), he made his pitch.

Whatever the critics said about the DB7, all agreed that it was beautiful. Callum's revisiting of the core themes as laid out by Ercole Spada were still valid, as the Vanquish project showed, and given the sales results for the DB7 (whatever some of the moaners in the AMOC had said) then the conception had been a commercial success. Bez's view was that this success should be reinforced. The replacement for the DB7 should therefore be more like it than not, but despite the budgets liberated and thus available within what Ford now referred to as the Premier Automotive Group (PAG), this was no time to reinvent the wheel.

Aston Martin had a very fine engine, which was proven. Aston Martin had tapped into a dormant and sensual design theme, recalling, but not aping, what will surely go down in history as the mid-20th century Milanese school, at which the entire industry, wrong-footed by boxiness, had swooned. Aston Martin also had, as Walter Hayes had discovered, a vast untapped resource of goodwill

Management changes

The cost of integrating Aston Martin into the Premier Auto Group was not merely financial. As the global economy tipped into recession and the stock market started to cascade at the turn of the millennium, the fortunes of the Ford Motor Company went with it. The collapse in confidence (car sales are unsurprisingly always one of the first casualties) in the wake of the terrorist attack on the World Trade Center in September 2001 only served to make a bad situation potentially catastrophic. For the fortunes of Aston to be yet again tied to the vagaries of commercial timing (as it had been when Gauntlett made his initial deal with Ford

just before the previous recession started to bite) was more than serendipity, for the central objective of Ford – to put its small portfolio of acquired brands (Jaguar, Aston Martin, Volvo and Land Rover) under a separately administered group – was the idea of Wolfgang Reitzle, supported by Jac Nasser. The simple truth, that such products require an entirely different approach to building and selling than do more modest products, was a lesson which Ford had learned with Mercury, but the effect on the careers of these men was more than serious. It was not the fault of PAG that Ford was losing money, but Nasser, the world-wide CEO, resigned shortly after the red ink was totalled, and many of the executives whose efforts he had sponsored went too, including Reitzle.

The DB9's muscular curves attract attention from any angle

Europe takes over?

Dr Ulrich Bez is the godfather of the DB9. Upon his arrival at Newport Pagnell in the summer of 2000, he was unsettled by the extant plans to change direction and produce a rear-engined car. He was able to convince Reitzle that continuity was the core issue and his conception of the VH platform not only made it possible to integrate Vanquish production with the new car, but would save an important amount of cash. With Reitzle's approval, Ian Callum went to work, and by August 2001, shortly before Callum's departure to pastures new, the outline of the DB9 was complete. In September 2001 Henrik Fisker, ex-BMW, replaced Callum and took over as design director to finalise the project.

The developments at Aston Martin were, of course, taking place at the same time as the unheard-of turmoil amongst Ford senior management, the most public outcome of which in the UK was the massive rationalisation of Ford UK production, particularly at Dagenham. The Unions were slightly miffed at the new working practices required before the move to Gaydon, and indeed there was some minor turmoil, which predictably made the front pages (Strike at Aston!); but, as one insider mentioned to me, 'I can't really blame them.'

Top: The DB9 exudes Aston Martin charisma.

Above: The hand-trimmed cabin is opulent, but classically simple.

Left: Dr. Ulrich Bez: godfather of the DB9.

Right: The DB9 Volante was given its world premiere at the 2004 Detroit Motor Show.

upon which to call. But the massive expense (and risk) in creating a new car, particularly a quick one, is the chassis, or platform as we must now call it. Aston Martin had survived, from the DB4 to the last V8 Vantage, on what was essentially the Harold Beach platform. It had been altered, widened, lightened, given a de Dion and so forth, and it had proved itself a truly worthy piece of kit, probably unique in motor car history. The DB7 had used an economically written-down Jaguar product and this has proved useful, if perhaps less than pin-sharp.

Bez's position was that a modular monocoque platform could be designed, which would contain within it everything that was known up to now for a conventional fore-and-aft front-engined layout. It would be known as the VH platform, V for vertical integration of the varied hardware it might carry up the range, H for horizontal integration across the resources of the Ford PAG. He knew it would be safe – Volvo would see to that. Bez was to build on the already close relationship between the marques which had been brokered by Hayes in the rationalis-ation of production techniques with both the Virage and its contempor-aries. The fact that Volvo was now part of the same umbrella organisa-tion would ease matters further.

So, Aston Martin installed its first robot. Its purpose? To connect up the various composite parts of the plat-form and body structure, built as it is out of a bewildering variety of materi-als (but mainly aluminium). This it does mainly by the use of glue. It is apparently known as the 'James Bonder'.

Commercially, the DB9 is important. It takes 200 hours to make one, but you wince when you realise that the DB7 took perhaps twice as long, and that with production targets of 5,000 a year.

This writer has yet to drive the DB9. Those who have, and whose other conveyances as road testers include all the usual suspects, concur that it may well be the best Aston Martin yet, which, if true, is a remarkable achievement. It is a fine example of what the best and the brightest of European engineering can do, given a benevolent parent.

Inflation adjusted, the DB9 is not significantly more expensive than the DB4 was when new. The ratio between it and the contemporary Jaguar is about the same, too, with Ferrari about where it was and Porsche reinvented. Maserati more or less disappeared but is now back with us, so there is a peculiar sense of déjà vu abroad in the land. The

question must be asked: who will be brave enough to put them all together on a circuit? One can only hope that production car racing will now be a serious possibility as a major spectator sport; Ford versus Fiat versus Porsche.

But even with the DB9 in full production, there is more to come; the next model to break cover has already been seen and no one will be surprised to learn that it is to be called the V8 Vantage. Powered by a 4.3-litre engine, it bears a close resemblance to the DB9/Vanquish family and, at a proposed 1,450kg (28.54cwt), but tugged along by over 380bhp of grunt, it is the closest thing to an entry level Aston Martin that we are likely to see.

With the V8 and V12 models, Aston Martin seems to have carved out its niche; the works at which these cars are now produced is by any measure a work of art in itself and, while the Vanquish will continue to be hand-built at Newport Pagnell, where the site is shared by the restoration/heritage operation, the historic Buckinghamshire site will seem to visitors to be very much unchanged.

But 60 miles up the road is where the future lies.

Acknowledgements

Despite the fact that this book is a personal view of the Aston Martin, there are many people whose help and co-operation have been invaluable.

Firstly, at Aston Martin Lagonda Ltd., I would like to thank Harry Calton, Kingsley Riding-Felce, Barbara Prince and the late Roger Stowers.

Outside the works, Richard Williams, Richard Zethrin, Vic Bass, Simon Draper, Stuart Briggs and Nigel Blanshard were all of immense help, as was my brother, Richard.

Thanks too to the Aston Martin Owners' Club, Aston Martin Heritage Trust, Haymarket Publishing and the LAT archive, all of whom have been most helpful.

Finally, I thank Alison Roelich and Flora Myer for their patience and all at Haynes Publishing, their editors, designers and staff, for putting up with the interminable delays which were, alas, unavoidable.

Index